# Acknowledgments

Many people contributed to this book in both small and big ways, it's nearly impossible to write a complete list. Many users of Power Pivot both inside and outside of Microsoft, bloggers, tweeps, conference attendees were my inspiration to finally start writing a book after almost 5 years of blogging. There already are some great books on Power Pivot out there but I think a real hands on and practical book on Power Pivot was needed.

Of course there are some people that I need to call out to as without their help this book or journey would never has started. I have to thank Rob Collie for those nights trying to understand DAX during the Project Gemini timeframe and urging me to go work for the Analysis Services team and change my life. John Hancock for believing in me and to teach me to never be afraid to think different and Julie Strauss for teaching me to challenge things and keep true to my gut feeling.

During the course of this book I have had the help of several folks inside Microsoft: Jay Thacker, Hassan Murad and Lance Delano for giving me that finance and business insight and giving honest feedback. The true masters of DAX: Howie Dickerman, Srinivasan Turuvekere, Jeffrey Wang and Marius Dumitru that helped me out when the DAX became too magical and clarity was needed (and check my formula's :) ). Amy, Russell and Drew to help me with the design aspects of the book. And lastly Ron Pihlgren for listening to my ramblings and helping me shape and review the book.

The writing of this books wouldn't have been possible without the help of Bill Jelen as publisher and Jocelyn Collie for the awesome cover design.

Finally I want to thank my family Mom and Dad for getting it all started with that first Commodore 64 :) and of course my beautiful girls: Anouk, Karlijn and Merel for putting up with my crazy passions and moving across the world with me to follow this passion.

# Dashboarding and Reporting with Power Pivot and Excel

## by

## Kasper de Jonge

**Holy Macro! Books**
**PO Box 82, Uniontown, OH 44685 USA**

# Dashboarding and Reporting with Power Pivot and Excel

Author: Kasper de Jonge

Layout: Tyler Nash

Cover Design: Jocelyn Collie

Indexing: Nellie J. Liwam

Published by: Holy Macro! Books, PO Box 82, Uniontown, OH 44685 USA

Distributed by: Independent Publishers Group, Chicago, IL

First Printing: March 2014. Printed in USA

Print 978-1-61547-027-3, Mobi 978-1-61547-118-8, PDF 978-1-61547-218-5, ePub 978-1-61547-339-7

# Contents

# Preface

Power Pivot and I were love at first sight, as soon as I installed the first beta of Power Pivot I knew the business intelligence world that I worked in would change forever. When I first installed Power Pivot I was working as a Business Intelligence consultant working on Microsoft SQL Server Analysis Services doing week or month long projects to give insights to large amounts of data to customers. Now with Power Pivot the same insights can be created directly inside Excel without having to be a Business Intelligence professional, being familiar with Excel is enough to create the insights you need. The enthusiasm of the BI professionals and Excel users alike to Power Pivot was incredible. In the years since Power Pivot has been released I have met a lot of customers both as a consultant and being on the Power Pivot team I have seen many scenarios where Power Pivot is very useful.

## Notes

This book covers a lot of different topics, written as a story about a user named Jim. Throughout the story, I often dive deeply into various subjects, call out certain areas, and give tips. To do this without deviating from the story, I make heavy use of notes, which fall into seven categories:

- Excel Tip notes
- Power Pivot Tip notes
- Dashboard Tip notes
- Power View Tip notes
- SharePoint Tip notes
- Power BI Tip notes
- General notes

The appendix provides an index of all these notes so you can easily find them at any time.

## Hyperlinks

Throughout the book, I reference sites and blog posts for further reading, including my blog, PowerPivot-Pro; Microsoft online help; and others. Because hyperlinks can be very long, I used a URL-shortening tool for the links I provide. For example, I would present the URL http://ppivot.us/SEUSO instead of the longer http://www.powerpivotblog.nl/project-gemini-building-models-and-analysing-data-from-excel-memory-based-dimensional-model/. Make sure you pay attention to the capitalization as you type the URLs as they are case-sensitive.

# 1- About This Book

This book is a little different from most books already out there on Power Pivot. It doesn't cover all the features of Power Pivot, nor does it cover the DAX language extensively. Many books before this one have already done those things well. Two good examples are Bill Jelen's *PowerPivot for the Data Analyst* and Rob Collie's *DAX Formulas for PowerPivot*.

This book is intended as a very practical book to help you get started on a Power Pivot journey that will bring your Excel and data analysis skills to the next level. This book follows Jim, a business user who is very familiar with Excel, on his journey to create a financial dashboard and complementary reports in Microsoft Excel. The journey starts with Jim finding out what information his organization needs in order to understand the current rhythm of its business. He then gathers that information and shapes it into a dashboard, in which he must determine the best ways to visualize information. As you follow Jim on this journey, you will use Power Pivot and DAX formulas to solve several very common business calculations, like year-to-date revenue, variance to target, and year-over-year growth.

You will also learn to create reports in Excel and Microsoft Power View to allow Jim's business to dive deeper into the numbers. Then you'll see how to share those workbooks to SharePoint and Office 365 Power BI.

In many places, this book dives deeper in subjects like the Power Pivot engine, DAX formulas, and Excel and dashboard design tips and tricks. Most of this book applies to both Excel 2010 and Excel 2013. However, Chapter 5 applies only to Excel 2013 because it's about Power View, which is not available in Excel 2010.

I hope you will find this book very useful in creating dashboards that provide insights into data, and I'm looking forward to seeing you out there in the Power Pivot community. You can find me at my blog, http://www.powerpivotblog.com, or on Twitter, at @kjonge.

## What Is Business Intelligence?

Before you get hands-on with Excel, it's important to look at why the tools discussed in this book even exist.

*Business intelligence* (BI) has traditionally been used as an umbrella term to refer to software and practice that should lead to better insights and decisions for an organization. Instead of making decisions based on gut feeling, an organization can base its decisions on actual facts it visualizes by using business applications. Many Excel professionals are likely to think, "Hey, that's what I'm doing every day, but I don't give it a fancy name!"

BI gained traction in the 1990s, when companies started creating and collecting more and more data but couldn't get the information into the hands of the business users to create insights and make decisions based on that information.

Building BI solutions has traditionally been the territory of IT organizations and consulting firms. It has often resulted in very heavy-weight and expensive projects; these highly curated and complex systems have brought together a lot of information from all over a company into a data warehouse.

A *data warehouse* collects data from all over a company and consolidates it into what many think of as "the single version of the truth." An IT organization may want all data to flow through the BI system to make sure it's consistent and non-redundant, in order to gain "correct" insights.

To make the data in a data warehouse actionable, organizations have often created *cubes* on top of the data warehouses. They have optimized these cubes to gain fast access to the data for doing quick analytics on large amounts of data. Organizations have created canned reports based on these cubes in order for users to get insight into the data. In the 2000s, Excel improved this situation, making PivotTables available, so users could drag and drop data from a cube straight into Excel.

Today, the stream of information that flows through an organization comes not just from BI systems but also from the number-one BI tool in the world: Excel. Users from the business side of an organization—not from the IT side—create Excel reports. These reports often bypass a BI solution completely or mash up data from the data warehouse with additional data retrieved elsewhere. This often causes IT and business users to clash because IT folks want the data to come from their BI solution, but the business cannot wait for IT to provide that information. The world does not stand around and wait for the data to become available. Events happen all the time, and it is often crucial for an organization to react quickly.

As the pace of the world has increased and as more and more data has become available to organizations, CFOs and other stakeholders in organizations have wanted to get insights into data faster and faster. BI traditionally was set to create insights through long projects, but that type of system makes it hard to quickly get insights into the data. When the recent financial crisis hit, the business world had to make many cutbacks, especially in the IT space. So at the same time that IT departments are expected to provide more insights and provide oversight over the data, they now have fewer resources to consolidate larger amounts of data.

But an organization doesn't need to rely on just its IT department for data. An army of Excel users in any business knows the data inside out, and they are very proficient at creating reports and using data to gain insights. What if Excel users and IT could work together to serve the information needs of the organization and use each other's strengths instead of competing? This was exactly the idea that started the self-service revolution in 2006 at the Microsoft campus in Redmond. At that time, Microsoft began an incubation project called Gemini, named for the constellation. The twins in this project are IT and business users, working together.

## The Self-Service Revolution: Power Pivot

Microsoft started its BI journey in 1994 by creating the very successful product Microsoft SQL Server Analysis Services (SSAS), which is designed for developers with an IT background. It is the bestselling analytical database engine in the industry. The idea behind Gemini was to shape the world-leading BI product SSAS into something that fits in Excel and can be used by Excel professionals. The Gemini incubation team aimed to determine whether it would be possible to empower Excel professionals and at the same time have them work together with IT. The team wanted to figure out how to put more business intelligence into the hands of the business users and allow them to "self-service" the information.

The Gemini team determined that it needed to create a product with a few radical features:

- **The ability to work with massive amounts of data:** Since SSAS hit the market in 1994, a lot has changed in the IT industry. Importantly, PCs have gotten more powerful, and memory has gotten much cheaper. What this meant for the Gemini team is that the product would need to work on the data and optimize it for analytics use in Excel. Whereas Excel 2010 and earlier allowed a user to work with 1 million rows of data, the Gemini team wanted a product that would allow users to work with very very large amounts of data directly in Excel—much larger amounts of data than anyone could have dreamed of before. The team thought that working with 200 million rows of data should be like a walk in the park.

- **The ability to create a single PivotTable that combines data from two separate tables without writing a single VLOOKUP()** —One of the most common uses of Excel is combining data from several separate data sources into a single report. In traditional Excel you need to use the complicated Excel function **VLOOKUP** to combine the data into a single table. In Power Pivot you can leave the data in the separate tables and just create a relationship.

- **The Data Analysis Expressions (DAX) language**—DAX, which is designed for analytics, is based on the Excel formula language and even shares some functions with Excel. At the same time, it's very different from the Excel formula language; whereas the Excel formula language references cells in a worksheet, DAX references tables and columns.

These three changes together bring a lot of power to the fingertips of many Excel users. As Bill Jelen describes in his book *PowerPivot for the Data Analyst* (http://ppivot.us/5Vqxd), "There are two types of Excel users: People who can do a VLOOKUP with their eyes closed and everyone else....Suddenly, hundreds of millions of people who (a) know how to use a mouse and (b) don't know how to do a VLOOKUP are able to perform jaw-dropping business intelligence analyses."

Project Gemini brings the power of SSAS to a billion users of Excel—right on their desktop. This is referred to as "personal BI" or "self-service BI."

But project Gemini is more than an add-in for Excel. A workbook can be shared with team members using SharePoint or Office 365. When it is shared, the workbook retains all the interactivity but can be used by many users at the same time, through a web browser (with no Excel required). The data in a workbook can be refreshed via an automated schedule so that new data is added to the workbook with no work needed! This is called "team BI." Sharing workbooks to SharePoint also allows IT to govern the data shared onto SharePoint.

In October 2009, Gemini was renamed *PowerPivot for Excel*, and it would ship with Excel 2010 (see http://ppivot.us/5Vd7u). It was quite clear that PowerPivot would radically change both business intelligence and Excel. Shortly after the release of Excel 2013, PowerPivot was given a space in its name—*Power Pivot* (http://ppivot.us/ifdYe)—and that is the term we use for the remainder of this book.

# Power Pivot Versions

As mentioned earlier, Power Pivot can be used with Excel on the desktop or in the browser using SharePoint or SharePoint Online in Office 365 and Power BI. In this chapter we take a brief look at each and see what the differences are.

## Power Pivot for Excel

Power Pivot is available for both Excel 2010 and Excel 2013:

- **Excel 2010**—When Excel 2010 was released, Power Pivot was first available as a free, download-able add-in for Excel 2010. The first version that shipped was called *PowerPivot 2008 R2*, also known as Power Pivot v1. In 2012 a follow-up version of the add-in, *PowerPivot 2012*, was released. This version can still be downloaded for free, from http://ppivot.us/Fmbg4.

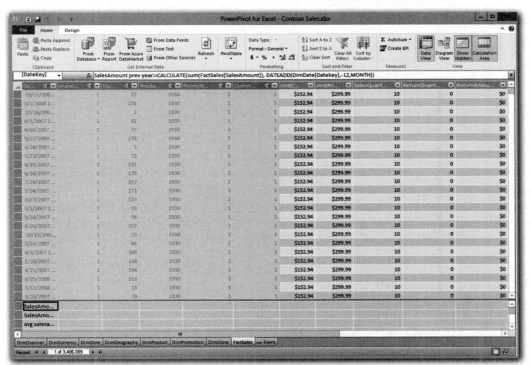

*Figure 1.1: PowerPivot for Excel 2010.*

> If you use Excel 2010, I highly recommend updating to the latest version of Power Pivot. Several enhancements made for later versions of Power Pivot have also been made available in this version.

- **Excel 2013**—With Excel 2013, Power Pivot no longer ships as a separate download from Excel but rather as part of Excel. Today it's available with the following versions of Excel:
    - Office Professional Plus
    - Office 365 Professional Plus
    - Excel 2013 Standalone

Both the Excel 2010 and Excel 2013 versions of Power Pivot are available in two flavors: 32 and 64 bit. The difference between the two has to do with the amount of memory Power Pivot can use on your machine. If possible, choose the 64-bit version of Power Pivot, which allows you to work with larger amounts of data. Not everyone has this luxury, though, as an IT department may centrally roll out the 32-bit version of Office for the entire organization, since most users don't need the 64-bit version of Office. Even though I prefer the 64-bit version, having the 32-bit version won't prohibit you from working with Power Pivot.

To see what version of Excel you are running, select File, Account, About Excel and look at the top right of the About window.

*Figure 1.2: Learning about Excel versions.*

All examples and screenshots in this book use Excel 2013, but almost all the functionality described here can also be used with Excel 2010. The exception is Chapter 5, which delves into building Power View reports.

## Power Pivot for SharePoint and Office 365

In order to share workbooks on SharePoint, an add-in to SharePoint needs to be installed on the Share-Point server. For this use, Power Pivot for SharePoint can be installed from a SQL Server installation medium. IT departments usually set up Power Pivot for SharePoint.

With the release of Office 365 Power BI, you can buy an Office 365 subscription that allows you to share workbooks to SharePoint for Office 365 without worrying about setting up an environment.

You'll learn more about sharing workbooks in Chapter 6.

# Tabular Models

In 2012 the SSAS team brought forward the Analysis Services Tabular Model. This is a version of Power Pivot that does not run inside Excel but runs on a server and is developed using the Microsoft programming tool Visual Studio. Most of the development is identical to that in Power Pivot in Excel, but it has some additional features that allow for working with larger amounts of data and that add security to the model.

This book focuses on Power Pivot for Excel and sharing these workbooks in either SharePoint or Office 365. For in-depth information on the Tabular Model, see *Microsoft SQL Server 2012 Analysis Services: The BISM Tabular Model* by Marco Russo, Alberto Ferrari, and Chris Webb (http://ppivot.us/3sblk).

## How I Got Started with Power Pivot

Today I work on the Microsoft BI team, which creates amazing tools that allow every Excel and business user in the world to gain insights into data. This is my story and how my love of Power Pivot brought me to work at Microsoft.

I have been passionate about computers and IT from the moment my parents bought me a Commodore 64 in 1988. Ever since then, I have been glued to computers, and when I started going to a school that focused on IT, I actually started paying attention, and my grades finally started going up.

*Figure 1.3: "Working" on my Commodore 64 in 1988. Look at that wallpaper.*

My first jobs were not in crunching data or getting numbers to people using Excel. I was riding the tail end of the dot-com bubble in the late 1990s, building websites. I've always had an affinity for trying to make sense of large amounts of data, but I had no idea there was a whole world out there that did this for a living—or that it had a name. I fondly remember that somewhere along the line, I tried to use HTML and SQL Server 6.5 to create a report that contained several charts. I continued going down the development path, using SQL, .NET, and ASP.NET while living in the weapon of choice for every developer: Visual Studio.

In 2004 I made a career switch to a DBA/developer role, where I was introduced to data warehousing, which I found to be like extreme database modeling. I was hooked instantly. Here I was also introduced to the tools that go on top of data warehouses, such as Cognos PowerPlay, which allows users in a business to analyze the data in their organization. I realized that users were able to get profound new insights, thanks to BI tools. They were enthusiastic about being able to work with such data for the first time.

When I decided I wanted to see some different companies, I tried my hand at consulting and moved back into a developer role. But I kept trying to get work that allowed me to give data to users in any shape or form. After about two years, I wanted back into business intelligence and managed to talk my manager into sending me off to an Analysis Services course. This five-day crash course in building multidimensional models was my introduction to Microsoft BI. After that, I largely focused on using cubes and reports and build BI solutions, as well as on occasional data warehouse jobs. I became a typical BI developer, working on long projects to deliver value to business users who usually had to wait some time to get the data they needed. They often came to my desk, asking for new calculations or additions to the models because they did not have the capability or tools to do it themselves. I wasn't really an Excel user, but I worked closely with business users (typically ones who did use Excel) to make sure they got the information they needed. While I was doing this work, I also started blogging, mostly to keep track of my findings for later reference. I still maintain that blog, at http://www.powerpivotblog.nl.

One day in late 2008, I heard about a new project called Gemini that would allow business users to gather and analyze their own data directly inside Excel (see http://ppivot.us/SEUSO). I was intrigued with this revolutionary technology that would bring the power of the complex cubes world to users directly inside Excel. This new product would make it possible for anyone in Excel to load millions of rows of data from multiple different places and combine the result into one report with ease. It seemed like science fiction to me then.

In August 2009, I finally got a chance to play with project Gemini and take it for a spin myself (http://ppivot.us/O1NUW). I was awed and in love. Gemini made it easy to quickly build reports that had before taken hours.

Then, in November 2009, my eyes were really opened, when I was introduced to the language that was underneath it all: DAX (http://ppivot.us/v3ThX). DAX is an incredibly powerful language that enabled me to do a lot with ease.

Around the same time, I found a partner in my Power Pivot explorations: Rob Collie (http://ppivot.us/aqdx8). We spent many nights trying to figure out how Power Pivot worked and trying to find new cool things we could do with Power Pivot. It was a pretty amazing time. I started trying to convince my manager that Power Pivot was a great tool and that we should use it in our day-to-day work with our customers; I was starting to get traction there.

In June 2010, I attended TechEd in New Orleans. Rob Collie and many other folks from the Microsoft Power Pivot product team were there, too. The conference was a frenzy of Power Pivot discussions. It seemed like this was the only thing the entire BI community could talk about. I had many discussions with Rob about Power Pivot, and near the end of TechEd, Rob said, "I'm leaving Microsoft. Why don't you take my job at Microsoft? I think you would do great." I was stunned. I'd never thought that was possible and dismissed the idea pretty quickly.

After some talks with my wife, I decided to send Microsoft my resume. A few weeks later, I was interviewing with the team, and about four months later, I had worked my first day at Microsoft, helping designing features for Power Pivot for SQL Server 2012. I was able to make a living from my hobby. Pretty awesome!

# 2- Introduction to Dashboards and Reports

In this book, you will learn how to build dashboard solutions in Excel and Power Pivot. Before you do that, though, let's start with some basics. The main goal of building anything in Excel is to display information from one or several "raw" data sources, either for your own use or to report the information to someone else. When you work with data for yourself, you don't have to think so hard about what it means because it makes sense to you. But when you build a data display for someone else, you have to think a little harder—to determine the reasons users request the information and what their goals are. You have to think about how to communicate the data so users understand it intuitively.

When communicating data, it's important to think about how to *show* and *visualize* the *relevant* information in an *efficient* way. Before you display a bunch of tables and charts, you need to think about why you use them. You need to consider whether to place one chart adjacent another chart. Most people don't think about this. This book looks at some real examples and investigates how to visualize information in an effective way, using some basic principles.

To determine how to display information, you need to think about the reason someone wants you to show that information. The answer will determine how you shape the data, usually in a report. The business intelligence world uses the term "report" to describe a mechanism for sharing information with users. The Bing dictionary tells a similar story for the term report: "(an artifact that) tell(s) about what happened: to give information about something that has happened."

Excel offers three main types of reports: dashboards, static reports, and interactive data exploration reports. There are times you need to use only one of them, but often they work together and complement each other. Let's look at what each of them means. Then, later in this book, you will use Excel 2013 to build a report of each type.

## Dashboards

*Dashboard* is a very loaded term in business intelligence and is often seen as being synonymous with BI. People seem to want or think they need dashboards without knowing what they really are or why they need them. But everyone seems to agree that dashboards look sexy and are cool to have. A dashboard promises to show all the information you need in a consolidated, simple, intuitive, clear, and car-like display.

Unfortunately, the average dashboard is a hotspot of flashy charts, traffic lights, and gauges that fails to deliver on the promise of information at a glance. The primary goal of a dashboard should be to deliver the right information in an insightful way. It should enable someone to spot the information needed at a glance. It's something a user looks at every day or even multiple times a day to see the current rhythm of the business and detect the areas that need immediate attention. Usually a dashboard contains information from more than one area. For example, it can contain sales, the number of new customers, and employee retention—all on one worksheet.

A dashboard should communicate the information you know the user needs very clearly at a level that is actionable and recognizable. For example, when a CFO is looking at sales, she probably doesn't need to see the sales for each product; she's more likely to just want to know if the organization is on target, and if it's not, she can call the product manager. The product manager probably wants to know which products are on target and which ones are not. These two individuals want the same information, but at a different level of detail.

Designing and creating a dashboard is hard not from a technical standpoint but from a design standpoint. If you ask someone what information he needs, he might tell you "everything." It's your job to distill the information to the right level; a dashboard cannot show all the information and should make sure to avoid information overload. You have to be scrupulous about what data you show: You have to pick the most important information in order for a dashboard to stay insightful. This means you need to really get to understand what information the user expects and needs in order for the dashboard to improve his day-to-day decision making. Great collaboration with your end users is necessary. A term often used to describe the information to display is *key performance indicators* (*KPIs*). Businesses often use KPIs to gauge the success or failure of key metrics in the business. As you create a dashboard, KPIs might give you a good starting point for gathering the right information.

As you think about the design of a dashboard, you need to answer a number of questions: How do you position the data on your worksheet? Is some information more important than other information? How do you visualize the information and then display it effectively? How do you use screen real estate as efficiently as possible? And how do you make the information on the screen actionable so the user can dive deep into the problems when needed? In Chapter 4 you will build a dashboard from scratch and look at how to display the right information.

## Static Reports

A *static report* is the type of report you are probably the most familiar with. Static reports are usually subject oriented and very detailed. They try to be exhaustive in terms of information and are meant for users who want to dive deep into a particular subject. Most companies run their business using static reports.

There may be several parameters that can be used to generate the data on a static report differently. For example, a report may be generated for a particular region or for all regions. A user can often access a static report from a dashboard when he wants to drill into more details in a particular area.

Static reports have traditionally been created in Excel or SQL Server Reporting Services, typically by either Excel or BI specialists.

## Ad Hoc Reports

*Ad hoc reports* give business users the flexibility to create and modify highly visual reports by using drag-and-drop. Whereas experts create the other report types, business users who don't need to be as tech savvy are the ones creating ad hoc reports. An ad hoc report should be quick to build and easy to use; the output should be highly visual and dynamic, telling a story that the business user wants to share. It should allow a user to derive great insights without having to rely on an expert. Microsoft allows users to create such reports by using Power View, which ships as part of Excel 2013.

# How to Determine What Information to Show

Before you can visualize or report any information, you need to make sure you understand what information you need to show. The creator of a report alone cannot determine what information to show. It's important for the report creator to understand what information the users of the report need in order to improve their insights into the business. This is usually done by interviewing the business users to figure out what they need. To show how this works, this book uses a fictional company, Contoso Communications, and tells the story of an employee named Jim, who is building a solution in Excel for his finance department to use.

## Getting to Know Contoso

Contoso Communications is a telco company that sells subscriptions and devices to customers throughout the United States. It is a very traditional company that has been around for 22 years and is mostly focused on traditional sales and services. It has 300 employees in several locations around the United States; most of these employees are in the sales and service department. Contoso Communications also has a small marketing and product management team. The finance team consists of 10 business analysts; Jim is a senior business analyst on this team. Contoso mostly outsources IT to external parties, except regarding some of the telco infrastructure. The company uses several systems, including ERP (Enterprise Resource Planning) and CRM (Customer Relationship Management) systems, but it doesn't have a consolidated data warehouse where it collects all the data.

Contoso Communications has had a difficult year, and the management team feels that it doesn't have a good enough grip on the information in the company. The team often reacts too slowly to changes in the business. The communication business changes rapidly. Each member of the management team needs to get a better grasp of the overall company numbers. All the team members also need to get more information about individual teams so they can react better to changes in the market. Jake, the CIO of the company, has been asked to come up with a solution for the management team.

Jim, who reports directly to Jake, has shown in the past that he is very proficient with Excel and Access. Jake has asked Jim to come up with a solution to allow the Contoso management team and finance team members to monitor the financial state of the company with ease, without having to search for relevant information in separate places. Jim is unsure what information needs to be shown, so he sets up time with each member of the management team and other key members of the financial team for an interview to take inventory of their needs.

## Interviewing the relevant business users

Jim starts by talking to Jake, who stresses the fact that Contoso Communications depends on a several core numbers that are very important to the day-to-day business:

- Overall revenue
- Number of units sold
- Usage of the devices
- Number of subscribers

In addition to these numbers, the management team wants to compare operational numbers with the targets that the business sets. The management team needs to see short-term numbers in order to react immediately. It needs to see long-term numbers in order to trend and predict where problems will arise in the future. At Contoso Communications, the fiscal year runs from July 1 to June 30, and the management team expects the information to be represented by fiscal year.

Members of the management team stress that revenue is by far the most important metric, and they want to be able to see the state of revenue for the company over time in order to see overall trends.

Jim also interviews one of his coworkers, Alice, who usually participates in management meetings. He learns that during their most recent meetings, management team members asked Alice to figure out why growth wasn't going as expected and whether it could be categorized in a certain way. Alice found out that the revenue growth was not equal for all regions; the management team determined that certain regions were underperforming due to marketing issues and was then able to take appropriate action. The management team now wants to keep an active eye on revenue by region to see if the revenue picks up again. The team wants to see the revenue to target for the current month and the trend over time.

One of the biggest ongoing efforts in the company during this fiscal year is trying to reduce the cost per unit. The management team wants to be able to see the results of cost reductions for the current period in order to see the results of these efforts.

Jim interviews Bob, the product management director who is responsible for products. Bob tells Jim that one of the things he wants to achieve is to reduce the number of products the company carries in order to save costs. He would like to see an overview of the best- and worst-performing products, by month, for the current fiscal year.

Now that Jim has interviewed the most important, relevant business users, he thinks he has enough information to move on. He has figured out what the management team considers to be the most important information, and he can start planning the dashboard and reports he needs to create.

## Planning the Dashboard and Reports

To begin planning his dashboard and reports, Jim creates a list of questions he needs to answer:

- What calculated fields do I need?
- What fields do I need to show on rows or columns?
- Where can I find the data needed to display the correct information?

Jim knows that answering these question won't give him a complete picture, but it will give him a good idea about what data he needs to produce and collect.

Next, he creates an initial inventory of the metrics he needs to collect, based on the interviews he conducted. This is what he comes up with:

- Sum of revenue
- Sum of units
- Sum of usage
- Sum of subscribers
- Sum of revenue target
- Sum of units target
- Sum of usage target
- Sum of subscribers target
- Revenue percentage of total

For each metric, Jim wants to be able to show that number against other metrics:

- Variance to target
- Year-over-year growth, as a percentage

Next, Jim needs to determine what rows and columns to use to show the metrics. He determines that he wants to see the values by:

- Region (country, region, state, city)
- Product
- Time (year, month, fiscal year, fiscal month, current month, past 12 months)

Now that Jim knows what he wants to show in his dashboard and reports, he needs to obtain the correct data.

## Obtaining the Necessary Data

Jim doesn't have all the data he needs at his disposal, so he goes over to the IT department to see what it can provide for him. The IT team can give Jim an export from several appropriate systems. This information will appear in an Access file that the IT team will update every week.

Now that Jim has collected enough information and has the data he needs, he can start building the dashboard and reports. In Chapter 3, you'll see what Jim does next.

# 3- Collecting and Preparing the Data

In this chapter Jim will collect the data needed for his dashboard by importing data from his data source and then prepare and optimize that data for analytics and visualization using Power Pivot for Excel 2013.

## Enabling Power Pivot for Excel 2013

Jim needs to show the first version of the dashboard to his manager in a few days. He just upgraded Excel on his desktop from Excel 2010 to Excel 2013 Pro Plus, using the company's Office 365 account. Jim is very proficient with Excel 2010 and Power Pivot, and even though there are many changes in Excel 2013 compared to Excel 2010, Jim's core Power Pivot skills will enable him to use the newer version of Excel without requiring too much new learning.

Jim opens Excel 2013 to start retrieving the data he needs for his analytics. He sees the ribbon but observes there is no Power Pivot tab on the ribbon.

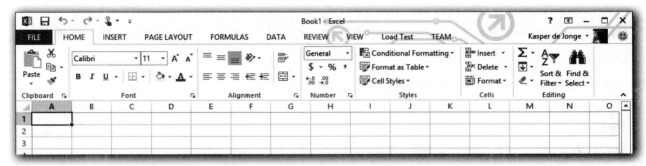

*Figure 3.1: The Excel ribbon.*

Jim needs to enable the Power Pivot add-in for the first time. To do so, he clicks File, Options. When the Excel Options dialog appears, Jim selects Add-ins, COM Add-ins, and then he clicks Go.

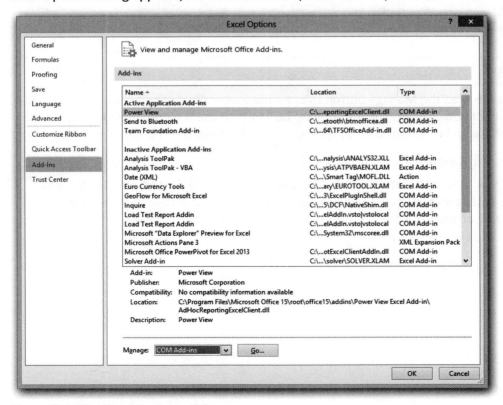

*Figure 3.2: The Excel Options dialog.*

In the COM Add-Ins window that appears, Jim selects Microsoft Office Power Pivot for Excel 2013 and clicks OK.

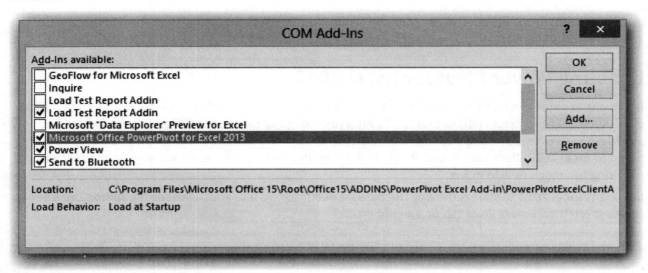

*Figure 3.3: The COM Add-Ins window.*

Now the Power Pivot tab is enabled inside Excel 2013.

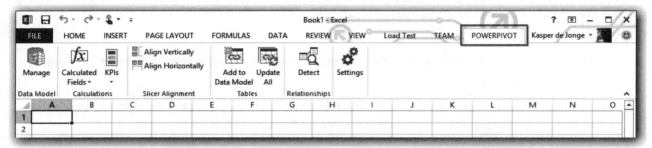

*Figure 3.4: The Excel Power Pivot tab of the ribbon.*

# Importing Data

Jim clicks the PowerPivot tab then the Manage button to open the Power Pivot window, where he has access to all the functionality of Power Pivot. The information he wants to use is stored in an Access file that is located on a network share on his network. At this point, Jim needs to import that data into Power Pivot.

### Power Pivot Tip: Supported Data Sources

Power Pivot allows you to import data from many sources, such as SQL Server, Access, Analysis Services, SQL Azure Database, and Oracle. Power Pivot uses data providers to import the data into the data model. During an import, you can choose from a large set of data sources.

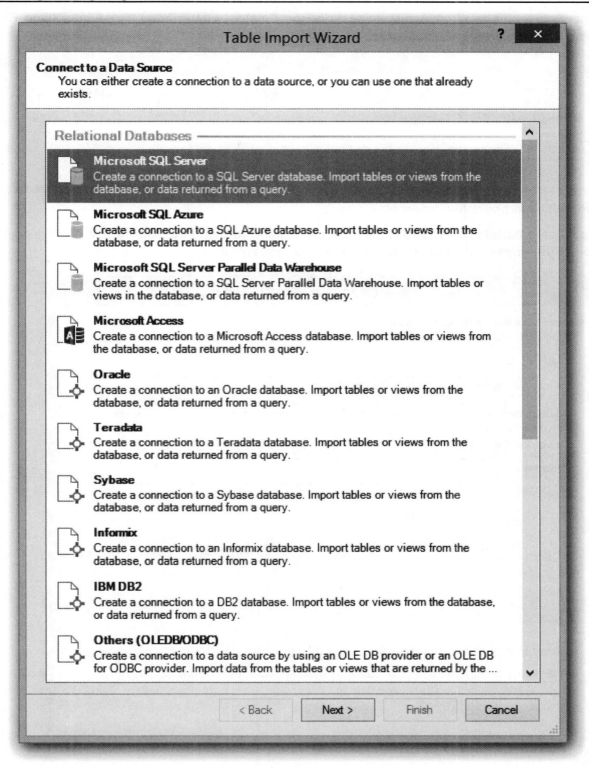

*Figure 3.5: Some of the data sources available in Power Pivot.*

Jim needs to get his data from Access, so he clicks From Database on the Power Pivot home ribbon, From Access. The Table Import Wizard appears.

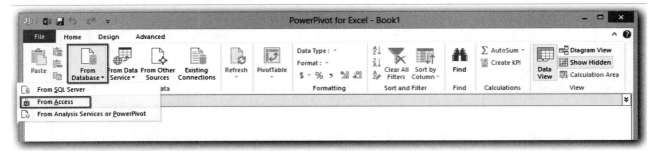

*Figure 3.6: Importing data from Access.*

Jim points the Table Import Wizard to the database he wants to import by browsing to it. This file does not require a user name and password, so he leaves those fields blank.

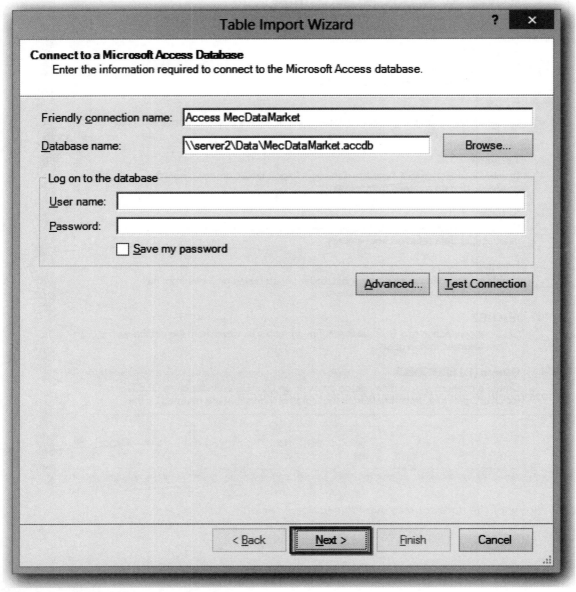

*Figure 3.7: The Table Import Wizard.*

Jim clicks Next, which brings him to the next step of the import process, where he has to choose how to import the data. He can choose to import through a query or by selecting individual tables. Jim chooses to import from individual tables and clicks Next again.

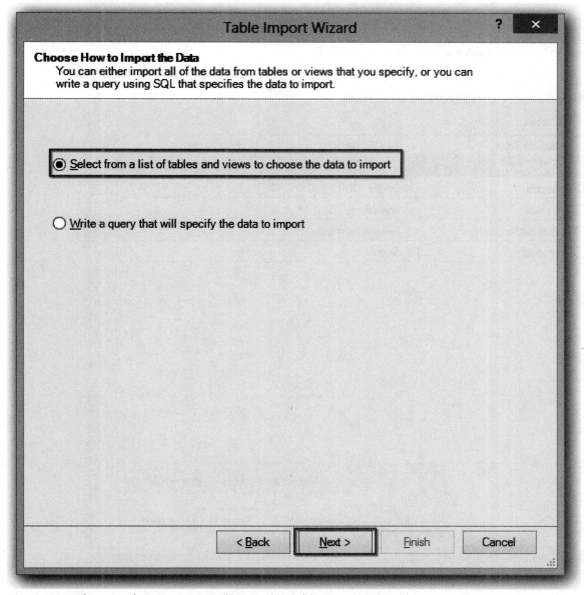

*Figure 3.8: Choosing how to import data in the Table Import Wizard.*

The next step in the wizard is a table selector. Jim needs all the tables shown in Figure 3.9, so he selects them all and clicks Finish to start the import.

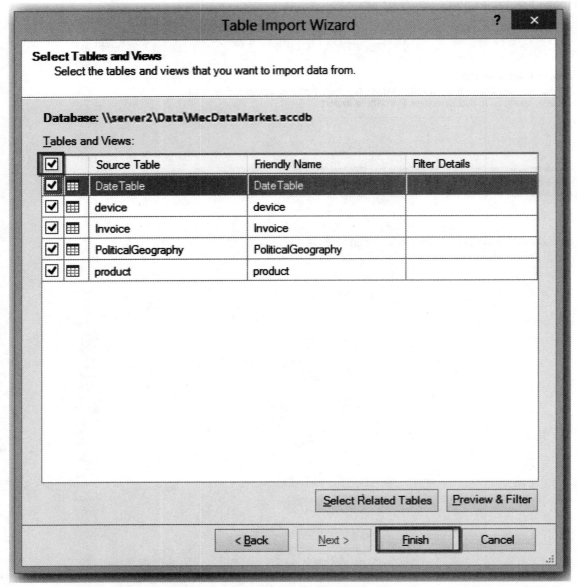

*Figure 3.9: Selecting tables in the Table Import Wizard.*

The data from the Access file is now imported. Together, the data from all these tables is called a Power Pivot data model.

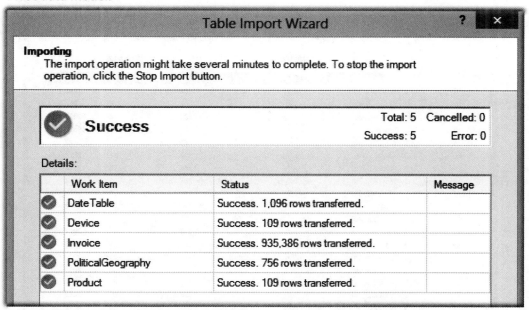

*Figure 3.10: Data imported into Power Pivot in the Table Import Wizard.*

### Power Pivot Tip: Storing Data

During a data import, the data is loaded into the memory of the computer that is running Excel. Power Pivot compresses the data by storing the duplicate values from each column only once in memory and replacing each original value with a small number that points to the real value stored somewhere else in memory. In Figure 3.11, colors indicate that values from each row are compressed in memory by replacing the value with a small numerical pointer value.

| ID | Year | Month | SalesPerson | Value |
|---|---|---|---|---|
| 1 | 2010 | January | Jeff | 34 |
| 2 | 2010 | January | Marty | 54 |
| 3 | 2010 | February | Jeff | 554 |
| 4 | 2010 | February | James | 23 |

*Figure 3.11: Visualizing compression in the data model.*

Compression is especially helpful when there are many duplicate values in the columns. Thanks to compression, large amounts of data can be loaded into a small amount of memory; you can even achieve tenfold compression rates. Thanks to this compression, data loaded into Power Pivot does not have a limit on the amount of rows, where data loaded in Excel has a 1 million row limit. Excel 2010 does have a memory limit of 2 GB that can be used for the model, Excel 2013 does not have a hard limit.

After the importing process is complete, the data grid view in Power Pivot shows all the data that was imported. For each table, it shows all the rows and the table structure (columns). Jim can switch between tables by selecting a table from the tab strip at the bottom of the window.

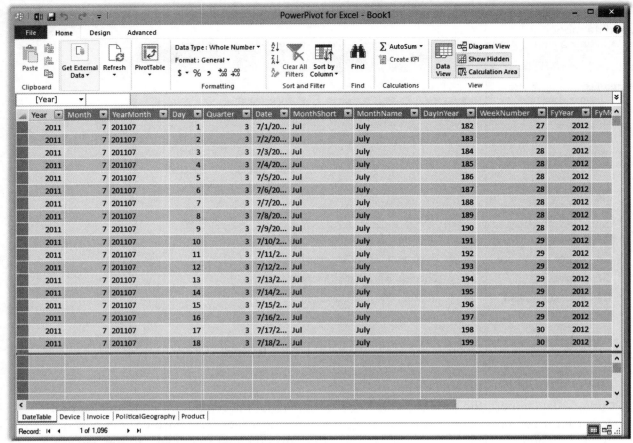

*Figure 3.12: The tables imported into Power Pivot.*

### Power Pivot Tip: Data Types

Another difference from Excel is that columns in Power Pivot are strongly typed. This means each column has a defined type, such as number or text. All values in a column have to be of the same type in order to be stored inside the data model. If this is not the case, Power Pivot throws an error. Some operations are not possible when data in a column is not the right type. For example, you cannot do a SUM operation on a text column.

One of the first things Jim does when he has the data loaded into Power Pivot is check the correctness of the columns in the Invoice table. He selects the Units column and notices that the data type is text.

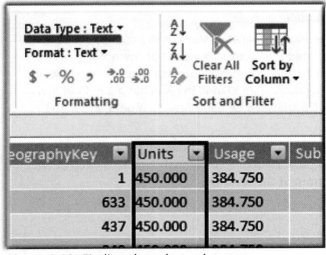

*Figure 3.13: Finding the column data type.*

Jim knows he wants to be able to use the Units column to summarize by time and by region, so he changes the data type for this column to whole number, which will allow him to use Units in an aggregation other than a count such as sum or average.

# Creating Relationships

Jim wants to combine data from different tables into one report. Instead of using `VLOOKUP` to consolidate all the data into one table, as is usual in Excel, Jim knows he can create relationships in Power Pivot.

In Power Pivot, Jim switches to the diagram view on the bottom right of the Power Pivot window (see figure 3.14). When the diagram view of the Power Pivot model opens, Jim can see the tables, their fields, and the relationships between tables. It's pretty clear in the diagram shown in Figure 3.14 that the columns are not related.

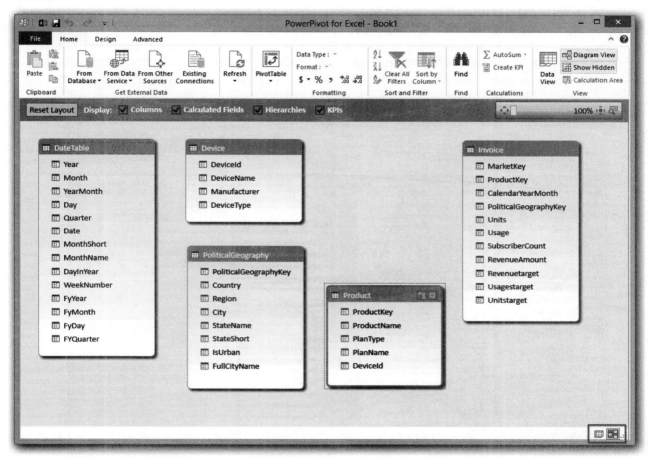

*Figure 3.14: Power Pivot diagram view.*

### Power Pivot Tip: The Power Pivot Data Model

Before you create any relationships in a data model, it is important to understand how relationships work in Power Pivot. In turn, to best understand relationships in Power Pivot, you need to look at the history of Power Pivot. Power Pivot is based on the SQL Server Analysis Services multidimensional engine. (For more information, see http://ppivot.us/DBRLO.) This product, created in the mid-1990s, is the leading MOLAP (Multidimensional Online Analytical Processing) engine in the industry, for more information see http://ppivot.us/IDCXA).

Analysis Services has served traditional BI developers and users of Excel connecting to cubes for years. These traditional business intelligence projects tend to use a star or snowflake schema—a design approach pushed by Ralph Kimball (http://ppivot.us/MPMZP) that has become the de facto design standard for data warehouses and cubes. The techniques and methods used in traditional data warehousing techniques shine through in Power Pivot. A Power Pivot developer who understands these techniques will be better able to design good Power Pivot models.

In the star schema, the model diagram looks (as you would expect) like a star. In this schema, the center of the star is called the *fact table*. The fact table describes the measurements, facts, or metrics of a business process. In Jim's case, the fact table is the Invoice table because it contains the invoices that are the metrics of Contoso's business. The center of the star is surrounded by dimensions. Each *dimension* is a descriptive table that describes attributes of a fact. For Jim, Product and PoliticalGeography are dimension tables that provide more details about the fact. Dimension tables are often reused between multiple fact tables and even multiple reports or cubes. Storing the data only once has obvious storage advantages.

Figure 3.15 shows Jim's tables rearranged into a star shape, with the Invoice table in the middle and the other tables around it. This arrangement is based on the keys inside the tables; for example, the Invoice table contains ProductKey, and the Product table also contains ProductKey. The ProductKey from the Invoice table is called a *foreign key*, and the ProductKey from the Product table a *primary key*. One single unique product has many different invoices for the same product. This is a one-to-many relationship, and it is the only type of relationship Power Pivot supports.

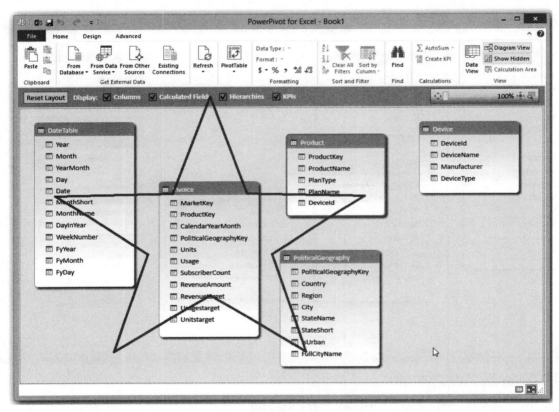

*Figure 3.15: The star shape in the schema.*

There is an outlier in this diagram: the Device table. This table is an outlier because it has no relationship with the Invoice table at the center of the star; however, it is related to the Product table. Because of this outlier, this diagram is actually a snowflake rather than a star.

Jim switches back to Excel and creates a PivotTable to test the data he just imported. He selects Data, Existing Connection to open the Existing Connections dialog, where he selects the Tables tab.

Figure 3.16: Selecting the model from the existing connections.

Jim now double-clicks Tables in Workbook Data Model. The Import Data dialog appears, and in it Jim can select how he wants to view the data. Jim selects PivotTable Report.

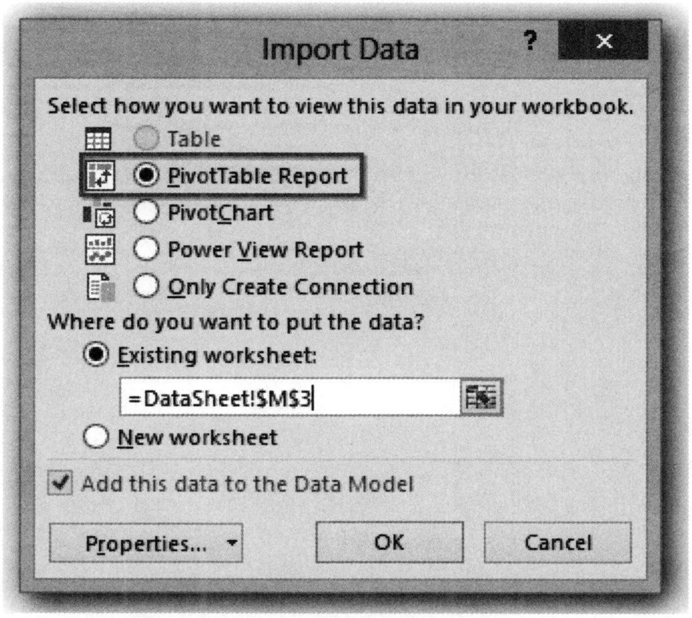

Figure 3.17: Selecting PivotTable Report.

Jim clicks OK, and Power Pivot adds an empty PivotTable to the worksheet. Thanks to compressions, data loaded into Power Pivot.

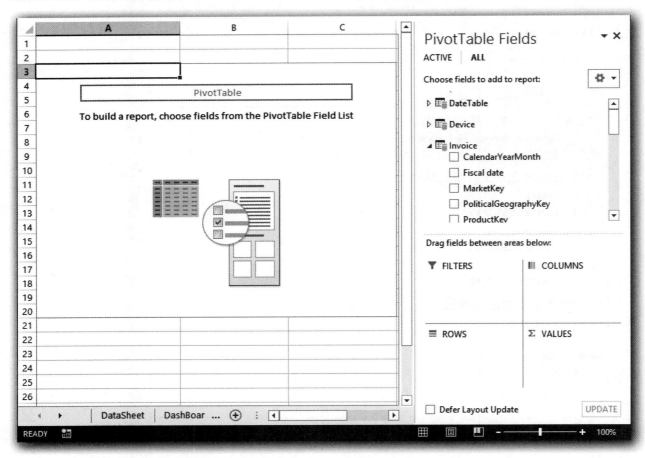

*Figure 3.18: An empty PivotTable.*

Jim tries to add values from two different tables into his PivotTable, but he gets incorrect results. He sees the grand total for each row in the PivotTable and a message in the field list that says "Relationships between tables may be needed." Power Pivot is unable to use values from different tables when no relationship is present. Jim needs to create them himself.

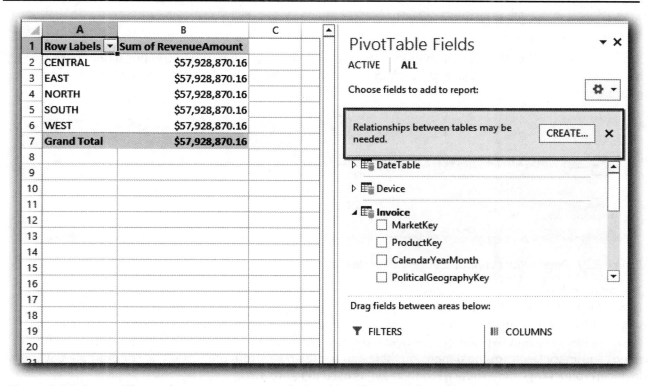

*Figure 3.19: Power Pivot asks you to create a relationship when one doesn't exist.*

Jim wants to create a relationship between the Invoice and Product tables. To do so, he opens the Power Pivot window and right-clicks the ProductKey column from the Invoice table and then clicks Create Relationship. The Create Relationship window appears.

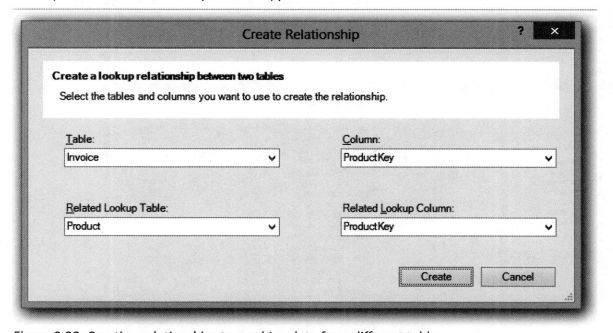

*Figure 3.20: Creating relationships to combine data from different tables.*

### Power Pivot Tip: Creating Relationships

As you can see in Figure 3.20, Jim has a ProductKey column from the Invoice table and a lookup column from a lookup table. In this case, the lookup table is the Product table, and the lookup column is ProductKey. *Lookup* is a great name to describe what happens with relationships. In this case, for example, Jim wants to look up the product information for each invoice. When re-

lationships are defined in the underlying data source, Power Pivot will create them automatically
for you during import.

Jim creates the rest of the relationships by dragging and dropping them. While creating a relationship
between the Invoice table's CalendarYearMonth column and the DateTable table's YearMonth column, Jim
gets an error.

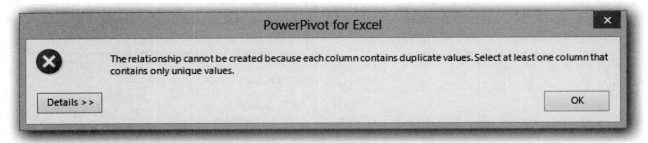

*Figure 3.21: Power Pivot cannot create the relationship.*

The relationship Jim has tried to create here is not a one-to-many relationship because the values of the
DateTable table's YearMonth column are not unique, as they need to be in a one-to-many relationship
where the column from the dimension table is a primary key. In order to be able to create this relationship, Jim needs to find two columns between the two tables that allow him to create this relationship: He
needs a primary key from the dimension table and a foreign key from the fact table. For example between
Invoice[ProductKey] and Product[ProductKey] as used in figure 3.20.

Jim uses the data grid view in Power Pivot to look at all the data in Power Pivot. He starts by looking at the
Date column from the Invoice table. When he clicks the arrow on the column, he can see all the unique
values from the column.

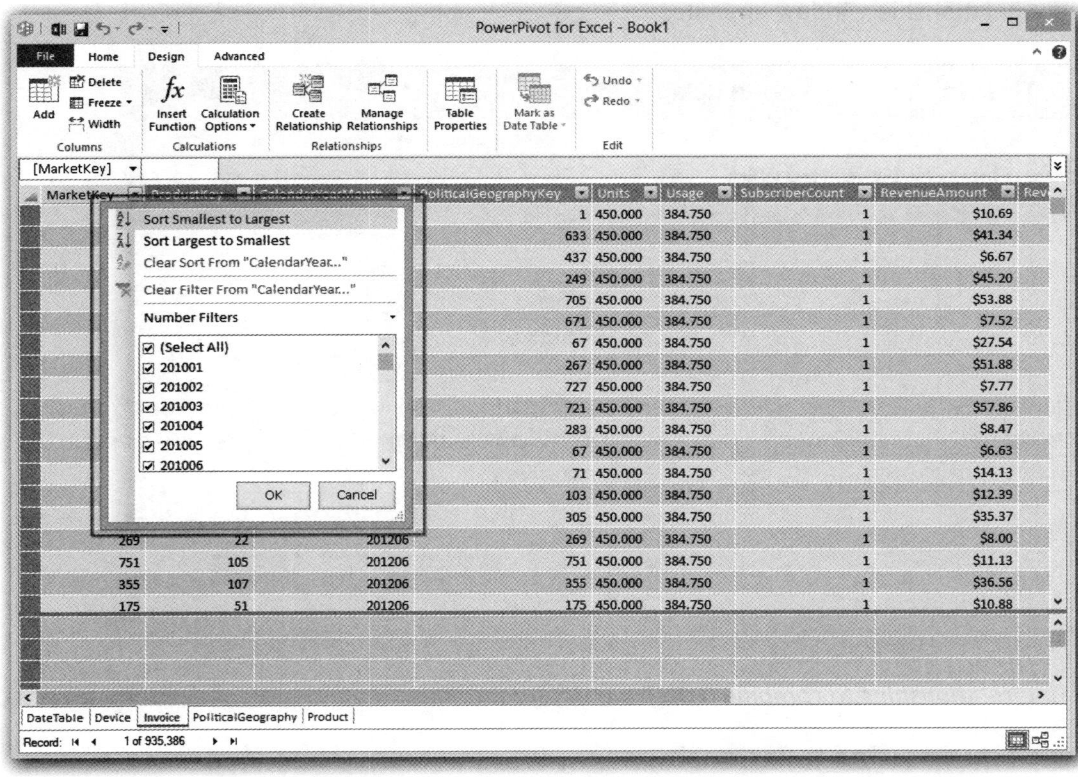

*Figure 3.22: Using the Power Pivot filter dialog to see the unique values in the table.*

Jim notices that the Date column in the Invoice table does not contain data on the day level but only has
values for each month of the year. Because this is the only Date column in the Invoice table, he needs to
use this column to create the relationship to the DateTable table.

Jim looks at the columns in the DateTable table. He needs to find the primary key, or the column that contains unique values for each row in the table. The only column that meets these criteria is the Date column.

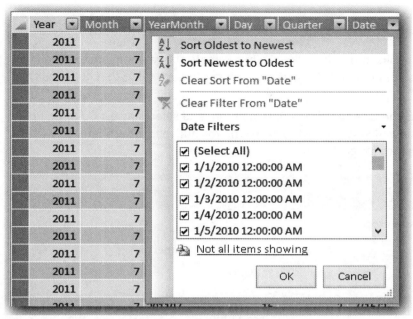

*Figure 3.23: Finding the unique dates in the column.*

In order for Jim to create a relationship between the Invoice and DateTable tables, the values from the two columns need to be identical. Jim can't change the Date column from the DateTable table to get rid of the date part of the value because doing so would make this value no longer unique for each row in the table. In order to create the relationship, Jim must create a field of the type date in the Invoice table by adding a day part to the CalendarYearMonth column of the DateTable table. In Excel, he could easily achieve this by creating a formula. Although you can't directly use Excel formulas in Power Pivot, you can use something very similar: DAX (Data Analysis Expressions).

### Power Pivot Tip: DAX Expressions

DAX is the formula language for Power Pivot. It looks like the Excel formula language and has many of the same functions, including DATE, SUM, and LEFT. Also like the Excel formula language, DAX uses a combination of functions, operators, and values in its formulas. But it has several distinct differences from Excel formulas. The biggest difference is that DAX doesn't reference cells or ranges but rather tables and columns in the Data Model. It is designed to work with relational data and to achieve very fast dynamic aggregations that utilize the highly optimized in-memory engine. DAX is designed for speed: It can quickly look up and calculate values across very large columns or tables.

There are two types of DAX expressions: calculated columns and calculated fields (also called *measures* in traditional business intelligence and in Excel 2010).

*Calculated columns* enrich tables. A calculated column in a table is based on a DAX formula. This DAX formula will be executed for each and every row inside the table, and the results of the formula will be stored in the table together with the values that came in during import. When you use a calculated column in a report, the columns looks and feels like it was imported into the model together with the rest of the columns of the table.

*Calculated fields*, on the other hand, are DAX expressions that you use in analysis when aggregating values of a column against a row or column in a report or PivotTable. For example, if Jim wanted to do a sum of revenue that he wants to pivot by each year or products, he would need to create an aggregation of the Revenue column from the Invoice table as a calculated field and use that in a PivotTable. The calculated field will be calculated for that PivotTable, the results will be calculated on the fly.

We'll look at many examples of both types of DAX expressions throughout this book.

# Enriching the Data Model with DAX

Jim wants to add a new column to his Invoice table that allows him to create the relationship to the DateTable table. To create the relationship, Jim needs to have one column in each table that contains the same values.

Jim selects the Invoice table, right-clicks the CalendarYearMonth column, and selects Insert Column. Power Pivot adds an empty column to the table and sets the text focus to the formula bar, where Jim can write a formula to populate the column with values for each row.

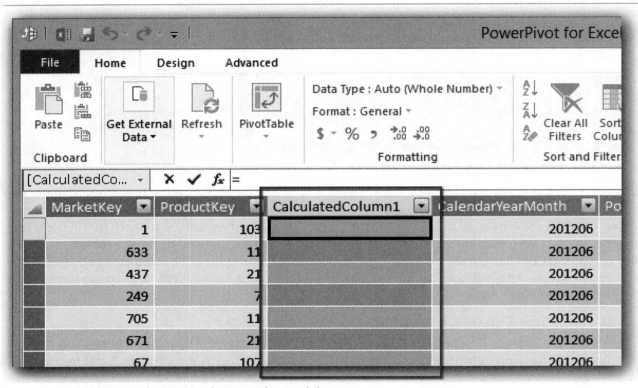

*Figure 3.24: Adding a calculated column to the model.*

In this case, Jim needs to turn the values from the CalendarYearMonth column into real dates. Just as he would in Excel, he starts typing =DATE ( into the formula bar. This gives him the results he is expecting, the autocomplete functionality tells him that this function requires three inputs: a year, a month, and a day. Jim knows how to get these values from the CalendarYearMonth string because the format is always 201206, where the first four characters are the year, and the last two are the month. These values don't include the day of the month, but Jim decides that he can just use the first day of the month for the purpose of relating the tables. He ends up entering the following DAX formula in the formula bar:

```
=DATE (
    LEFT([CalendarYearMonth],4)
    , RIGHT([CalendarYearMonth],2)
    , 1)
```

Jim presses Enter, and the formula executes.

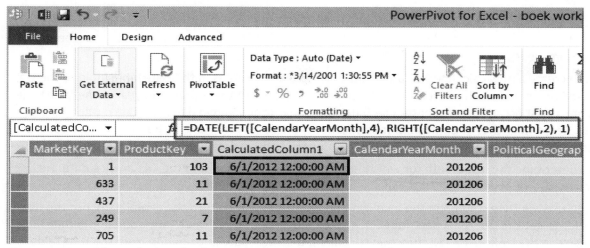

Figure 3.25: With a calculated column, the formula is evaluated for each row in the table.

## Power Pivot Tip: Calculated Columns

Jim is used to copying formulas to all the rows in a table in Excel. However, Power Pivot automatically applies a formula to all the rows in the table. In the expression, the reference to other columns in the same table automatically returns the value for that column in the row where the formula is executed.

Jim is happy. He has a column that contains dates that he can use to create a relationship to the DateTable table. By default, this new column is called CaculatedColumn1; Jim double-clicks the header of the column, which will allow him to rename this column to Date. Jim now opens the diagram view to create a relationship between the Invoice and DateTable table. He selects the date field from Invoice table and drags it to date field of the DateTable, this will create the relationship between the two tables. Jim also creates relationship for all the tables that don't have a relationship yet. The diagram with all the relationships looks as shown in Figure 3.26. The lines between the tables indicate the relationships that between the tables.

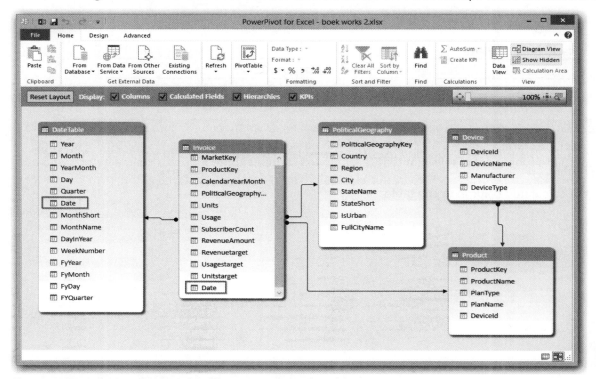

Figure 3.26: Relationships created between multiple tables.

## Selecting the Current Fiscal Month and Year

The next thing Jim wants to do is create a column in the DateTable table that he can use to filter his reports and automatically return data for the current fiscal year or month (that is, the last fiscal year or month for which he has invoices).

Jim needs to create a new calculated column that compares all the dates in the DateTable table to the last fiscal date for which he has an invoice; the column should return 1 if the month and year in the DateTable are the same as last fiscal year or month. The DateTable table contains two different dates: calendar and fiscal dates. Remember that at Contoso Communications, the fiscal year runs from July 1 to June 30; therefore, when the normal calendar date is 11/30/2012, Contoso's fiscal date is 5/31/2013.

In order to determine the last month for which he has data, Jim needs to find the last invoice date. He decides to create a calculated field to get this date so that he can reuse that value in other places.

Jim wants to use the Date column in the Invoice table, but that would return the actual date, not the fiscal date. In order to get the last fiscal date for each invoice, Jim can leverage the information in the DateTable table. He can use the DAX RELATED function to look up the fiscal date information from the DateTable table for each invoice date by using the table relationship. In the Invoice table, Jim adds a column with the following expression:

```
=DATE (
    RELATED(DateTable[FyYear])
    ,RELATED(DateTable[FyMonth])
    ,1
    )
```

This formula uses the DATE function to create a date value in the Invoice table. The DATE function expects three arguments: a year, a month, and a day. Jim uses the RELATED function to get the FyYear and FyMonth values from the DateTable table. The RELATED function then uses the relationship between the tables to get the values from the DateTable table for each row in the Invoice table.

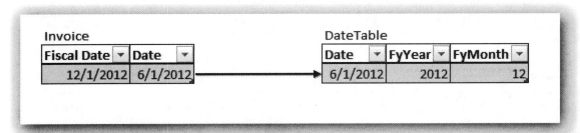

*Figure 3.27: The RELATED function uses the relationship between tables to get values from the other table.*

This adds the calculated column to the table:

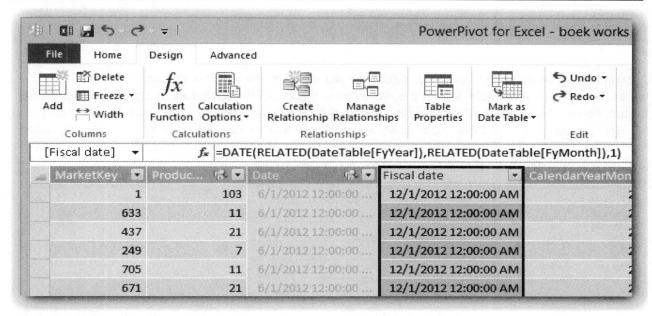

*Figure 3.28: The values from the calculated column are added for each row*

Jim now hides the Fiscal date and Date columns in the Invoice table, they are just to create the relationships. For use of dates in the PivotTable Jim needs to use the values in the DateTable.

> A column can be hidden by right mouse clicking on the column and selecting "Hide from Client Tools" (see figure 3.40). The hidden column is recognizable when the column is greyed out in the data grid view, take a look at the date column in figure 3.29.

Jim is ready to create a calculated field to select the last invoice fiscal date. He selects the Invoice table and highlights an empty spot in the calculation area.

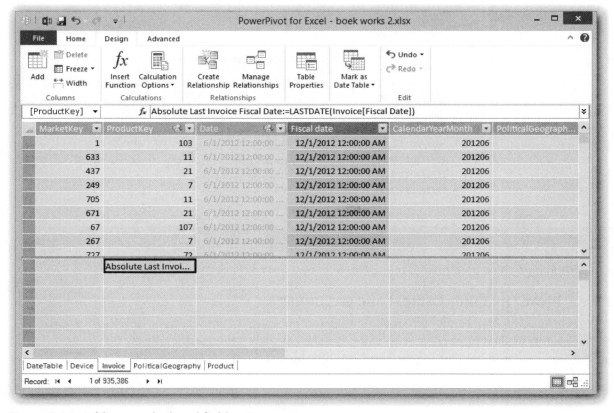

*Figure 3.29: Adding a calculated field to Power Pivot.*

He enters the following formula in the selected spot:

```
[Absolute Last Invoice Fiscal Date]=
        LASTDATE(Invoice[Fiscal Date])
```

Jim wants this calculated field to always return the last date for which he has an invoice. To test that it works, he creates a PivotTable, selects the Home tab in the Power Pivot window, and clicks the PivotTable button. Power Pivot creates a PivotTable in Excel. In the PivotTable Fields pane, Jim adds FyYear and Fy-Month from the DateTable table under Rows, and he adds the Absolute Last Invoice Fiscal Date calculated field under Values. Unfortunately, this doesn't give Jim the results he expected: Instead of returning the last invoice fiscal date ever, it returns the last invoice fiscal date for *each* month in the PivotTable.

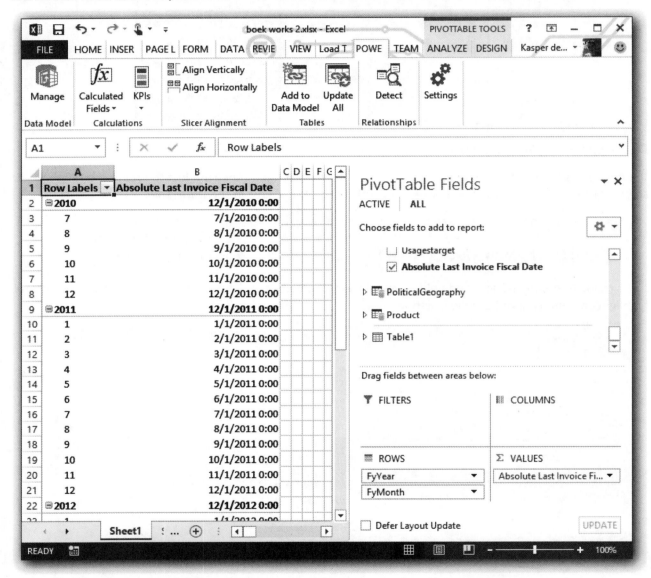

*Figure 3.30: Adding a calculated field to a PivotTable allows Jim to check the end result.*

### Power Pivot Tip: Filter Context and CALCULATE

DAX returns values filtered by whatever is selected on rows, columns, filters, or slicers. In DAX, this behavior is called *filter context*. In this case, the calculated field automatically filters the values of the calculated field for FyYear and FyMonth that are on the rows of the PivotTable.

| | A | B | C | D | E |
|---|---|---|---|---|---|
| 1 | Row Labels ▼ | Absolute Last Invoice Fiscal Date | | | |
| 2 | ⊟ 2010 | 12/1/2010 0:00 | | | |
| 3 | 7 | 7/1/2010 0:00 | | | |
| 4 | 8 | 8/1/2010 0:00 | | | |
| 5 | 9 | 9/1/2010 0:00 | | | |
| 6 | 10 | 10/1/2010 0:00 | | | |
| 7 | 11 | 11/1/2010 0:00 | | | |
| 8 | 12 | 12/1/2010 0:00 | | | |
| 9 | ⊟ 2011 | 12/1/2011 0:00 | | | |
| 10 | 1 | 1/1/2011 0:00 | | | |
| 11 | 2 | 2/1/2011 0:00 | | | |
| 12 | 3 | 3/1/2011 0:00 | | | |

*Figure 3.31: In the two highlighted rows, the* `LASTDATE` *formula returns only the last date for the month selected in the PivotTable.*

Because filter context is the single most important concept in DAX, I want to spend a little time making sure you understand it, so consider a simple example. Imagine creating a calculated field, like so:

```
[Sum of RevenueAmount]=
        SUM(Invoice[RevenueAmount])
```

This calculated field will add all the numbers in a column called Invoice[RevenueAmount]. But based on what? Look at what happens when you put that calculated field in a PivotTable.

| Sum of RevenueAmount |
|---|
| $57,928,870.16 |

*Figure 3.32: Just a calculated field inside a PivotTable.*

When you put a calculated field in a PivotTable without any fields on rows or columns, you get the value for all the values of the Invoice[RevenueAmount] column for the entire table; that is, no filter is applied to the value. Now look at what happens when you add regions to rows.

| Row Labels ▼ | Sum of RevenueAmount |
|---|---|
| CENTRAL | $5,144,564.75 |
| EAST | $22,990,559.38 |
| NORTH | $12,666,250.34 |
| SOUTH | $4,777,531.71 |
| WEST | $12,349,963.98 |
| Grand Total | $57,928,870.16 |

*Figure 3.33: The same calculated field now shows a result for each region.*

You expected this behavior to happen, right? The values are now split out by region, with one grand total. How does this work? What happens here is that the same Sum of RevenueAmount calculated field is calculated six times: once with a filter on each region and once for the grand total. You can make it a little bit more interesting, as shown in Figure 3.34.

| Sum of RevenueAmount | Column Labels | | | | |
|---|---|---|---|---|---|
| Row Labels | 2010 | 2011 | 2012 | 2013 | Grand Total |
| CENTRAL | $864,235.25 | $1,676,786.45 | $1,782,040.90 | $821,502.14 | $5,144,564.75 |
| EAST | $4,521,114.19 | $8,021,793.31 | $7,341,430.87 | $3,106,221.00 | $22,990,559.38 |
| NORTH | $2,106,381.13 | $4,108,185.26 | $4,407,871.72 | $2,043,812.22 | $12,666,250.34 |
| SOUTH | $801,032.30 | $1,556,195.67 | $1,618,571.93 | $801,731.81 | $4,777,531.71 |
| WEST | $2,058,417.70 | $4,007,433.24 | $4,286,573.08 | $1,997,539.95 | $12,349,963.98 |
| Grand Total | $10,351,180.58 | $19,370,393.94 | $19,436,488.51 | $8,770,807.12 | $57,928,870.16 |

Figure 3.34: More values on rows and columns means the calculated field is executed more times.

Here the filter context for each cell in the PivotTable is more complex. For example, when you look at Sum of RevenueAmount for FyYear 2012 and Region North, you see a single cell in the PivotTable that is filtered by FyYear 2012 and Region North.

| Sum of RevenueAmount | Column Labels | | | | |
|---|---|---|---|---|---|
| Row Labels | 2010 | 2011 | 2012 | 2013 | Grand Total |
| CENTRAL | $864,235.25 | $1,676,786.45 | $1,782,040.90 | $821,502.14 | $5,144,564.75 |
| EAST | $4,521,114.19 | $8,021,793.31 | $7,341,430.87 | $3,106,221.00 | $22,990,559.38 |
| NORTH | $2,106,381.13 | $4,108,185.26 | $4,407,871.72 | $2,043,812.22 | $12,666,250.34 |
| SOUTH | $801,032.30 | $1,556,195.67 | $1,618,571.93 | $801,731.81 | $4,777,531.71 |
| WEST | $2,058,417.70 | $4,007,433.24 | $4,286,573.08 | $1,997,539.95 | $12,349,963.98 |
| Grand Total | $10,351,180.58 | $19,370,393.94 | $19,436,488.51 | $8,770,807.12 | $57,928,870.16 |

Figure 3.35: The value of Sum of RevenueAmount for FyYear 2012 is filtered by Region North.

What does this mean? Remember that all calculated fields are filtered by whatever is put on rows, columns, filters, and slicers; this is the *filter context* of a calculated field. Imagine the filter context as a small submodel with data filtered by the values on rows/columns/filters or slicers context. This is the most important fundamental concept to grasp in Power Pivot, so you need to be sure you understand it.

Very importantly, you can put this behavior to use with DAX. Certain DAX functions allow you to tell the DAX engine to ignore a filter set by a report but to instead always use whatever you tell it to use.

The most powerful function in DAX is the CALCULATE function, which you use like this:

```
CALCULATE(<expression>,<filter1>,<filter2>...)
```

Here's what MSDN (http://ppivot.us/ub50Z) says about this function: "Evaluates an expression in a context that is modified by the specified filters." In other words, the CALCULATE function allows you to execute an expression and to express your own filters. Here's an example:

```
[Sum of RevenueAmount CALC]=
        CALCULATE(
                SUM([RevenueAmount])
                ,PoliticalGeography[Region]="North")
```

Here you tell the Power Pivot engine to set the filter of the SUM([RevenueAmount]) expression to PoliticalGeography[Region]="North", and in Figure 3.36 you can see what it looks like when you put this calculated field on a PivotTable.

| Sum of RevenueAmount CALC | Column Labels | | | | |
|---|---|---|---|---|---|
| Row Labels | 2010 | 2011 | 2012 | 2013 | Grand Total |
| CENTRAL | $2,106,381.13 | $4,108,185.26 | $4,407,871.72 | $2,043,812.22 | $12,666,250.34 |
| EAST | $2,106,381.13 | $4,108,185.26 | $4,407,871.72 | $2,043,812.22 | $12,666,250.34 |
| NORTH | $2,106,381.13 | $4,108,185.26 | $4,407,871.72 | $2,043,812.22 | $12,666,250.34 |
| SOUTH | $2,106,381.13 | $4,108,185.26 | $4,407,871.72 | $2,043,812.22 | $12,666,250.34 |
| WEST | $2,106,381.13 | $4,108,185.26 | $4,407,871.72 | $2,043,812.22 | $12,666,250.34 |
| Grand Total | $2,106,381.13 | $4,108,185.26 | $4,407,871.72 | $2,043,812.22 | $12,666,250.34 |

*Figure 3.36: Setting the filter argument of CALCULATE overrides any outside filters.*

If you compare Figure 3.36 with Figure 3.35, you can see that the same row is repeated for each region—in this case the region North—but it is very important to observe that the FyYear column values are still filtered appropriately. So as soon as you add a field to the filter argument, any "outside" filters on this field will be ignored, and the ones added to the calculated field will be used instead.

Here's one more example:

```
[Sum of RevenueAmount CALC]=
    CALCULATE(
            SUM([RevenueAmount]),
            ALL(PoliticalGeography[Region]))
```

In this case, you tell the Power Pivot engine to set the filter of the SUM([RevenueAmount]) expression to *all* values of PoliticalGeography[Region], effectively removing the filter each time the calculated field is executed.

| Sum of RevenueAmount CALC | Column Labels | | | | |
|---|---|---|---|---|---|
| Row Labels | 2010 | 2011 | 2012 | 2013 | Grand Total |
| CENTRAL | $10,351,180.58 | $19,370,393.94 | $19,436,488.51 | $8,770,807.12 | $57,928,870.16 |
| EAST | $10,351,180.58 | $19,370,393.94 | $19,436,488.51 | $8,770,807.12 | $57,928,870.16 |
| NORTH | $10,351,180.58 | $19,370,393.94 | $19,436,488.51 | $8,770,807.12 | $57,928,870.16 |
| SOUTH | $10,351,180.58 | $19,370,393.94 | $19,436,488.51 | $8,770,807.12 | $57,928,870.16 |
| WEST | $10,351,180.58 | $19,370,393.94 | $19,436,488.51 | $8,770,807.12 | $57,928,870.16 |
| Grand Total | $10,351,180.58 | $19,370,393.94 | $19,436,488.51 | $8,770,807.12 | $57,928,870.16 |

*Figure 3.37: Using ALL as a filter in CALCULATE has the effect of removing the filter for each cell.*

Filter context and the CALCULATE function are your main tools for getting the most out of Power Pivot and DAX. DAX Formulas for Power Pivot by Rob Collie goes into more details on filter context: http://ppivot.us/gYukh

Jim changes his calculated field to make sure the last date of the entire table is calculated:

```
[Absolute Last Invoice Fiscal Date]=
    CALCULATE(
        LASTDATE(Invoice[Fiscal Date])
        , ALL(Invoice)
        )
```

By using CALCULATE and ALL, you tell the engine to always calculate the last date of the In-voice[Date] column for all the rows in the Invoice table, thus ignoring any filters.

Jim goes back to his PivotTable and observes that the same value now is returned for all the rows in the PivotTable.

| | A | B |
|---|---|---|
| 1 | Row Labels ▼ | Absolute Last Invoice Fiscal Date |
| 2 | ⊟ 2010 | 5/1/2013 0:00 |
| 3 | 7 | 5/1/2013 0:00 |
| 4 | 8 | 5/1/2013 0:00 |
| 5 | 9 | 5/1/2013 0:00 |
| 6 | 10 | 5/1/2013 0:00 |

*Figure 3.38: The last date is now calculated for the entire Invoice table.*

Now Jim needs to add to the DateTable a new column that he can use in his filters to select the current fiscal year. He creates two new calculated columns in the DateTable table to check the current fiscal year:

```
[CurrentFyYear]=
    IF(
        [FyYear]=YEAR([Last Invoice Fiscal Date])
        ,1
        ,0
    )
```

This calculated column returns 1 if the value from the FyYear column is the same as the year part returned by the [Last Invoice Fiscal Date] calculated field.

And a similar function adds a column that returns 1 when the DateTable row is the current fiscal month:

```
[CurrentFyMonth]=
    IF(
        [FyYear]=YEAR([Last Invoice Fiscal Date])
        &&
        [FyMonth]=MONTH([Last Invoice FyDate])
        ,1
        ,0
    )
```

These calculated columns compare the values from the current FyYear and FyMonth columns in the DateTable table with the Year and Month returned by the [Last Invoice Fiscal Date] calculated field. If the values are the same, the calculated field returns 1; otherwise, it returns 0.

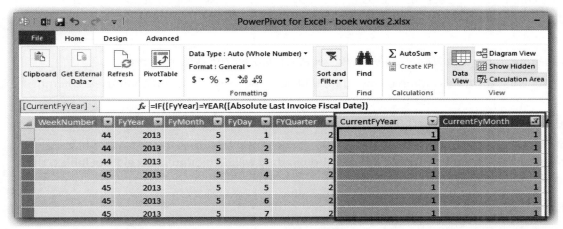

*Figure 3.39: The formulas in the calculated columns will be evaluated every time the data is refreshed.*

## Working with Time Calculations

Now that he has created the relationships and enriched the data model with additional columns, Jim can focus on other aspects of the model that he needs to add in order to get the results requested by the business. Jim has anticipated that he needs to add many calculated fields that are date related—for example, calculations using running total, previous month, and year to date.

### Power Pivot Tip: The Time Intelligence Functions

DAX contains many functions that make working with time easier. These functions are called the *time intelligence functions*.

Working with the time intelligence functions can be quite difficult for a novice DAX user. To make working with these functions easier, you can apply a set of "golden rules" to any workbook:

1. *Never use a date column from a fact table as a date arguments in time intelligence functions.*

Remember the filter context concept discussed a little bit ago? Imagine that you add years to the rows of your PivotTable. Power Pivot would automatically filter the row context down to contain only values of that year. If you then want to compare with a previous year, you need to overwrite that filter context. This is possible with DAX but can quickly become very cumbersome. When you follow this rule—and avoid using *a* date column from a fact table as a date column in DAX time functions—you don't have to worry about this issue because the functions will take care of overriding the filters.

2. *Always create a separate date table.*

The date table should consist of at least a date column that covers the first and last dates you want to report on and any columns that you want to use in your report, such as year and month. This is usually the date argument that you can use with your time intelligence functions.

3. *Make sure your date table includes a continuous date range.*

DAX uses the date column to navigate through time. Say that you have selected January 2013 in a PivotTable, and you want to show the sales for last year. DAX will automatically determine the date range for January 2013 using your date table, then it will use that date range to determine the date range for January 2012. Now if the date table is missing some dates in January 2013, that same day will be missing for the previous year that might have some sales that are now missing.

4. *Create relationships between fact tables and the date table.*

Using the relationships you can use values from the date table in your PivotTable.

5.  *The date column in the date table should be at day granularity (without fractions of a day).*

DAX doesn't support dates smaller than the day granularity. It is often a good idea to remove the time parts of dates for performance and compression reasons.

6.  *Mark the date table as a "Date Table" in Power Pivot and set the Date column.*

This tells DAX what the date column of your date table is, especially when you don't use a column of date data type to create your relationship.

For more information, see http://ppivot.us/DYBUJ.

Jim selects both date columns from the Invoice table and hides them. He does this to ensure that he doesn't use the date fields from the Invoice table. Although they will be hidden in Excel PivotTables, they can still be used in DAX formulas.

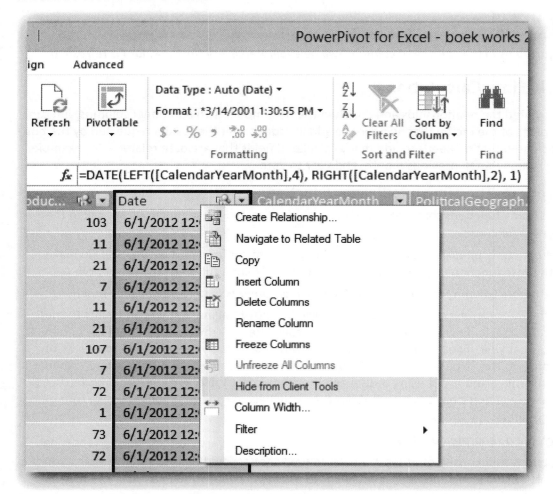

*Figure 3.40: Always hide columns that you think you will not use in a report.*

Jim plans to use the DateTable table that is available in his data source because it meets all the requirements. He has also created a relationship between the DateTable table and his fact table. Jim selects the DateTable table and then selects Design, Mark as Date Table. In the Mark as Date Table dialog that appears, he selects the Date column and clicks OK.

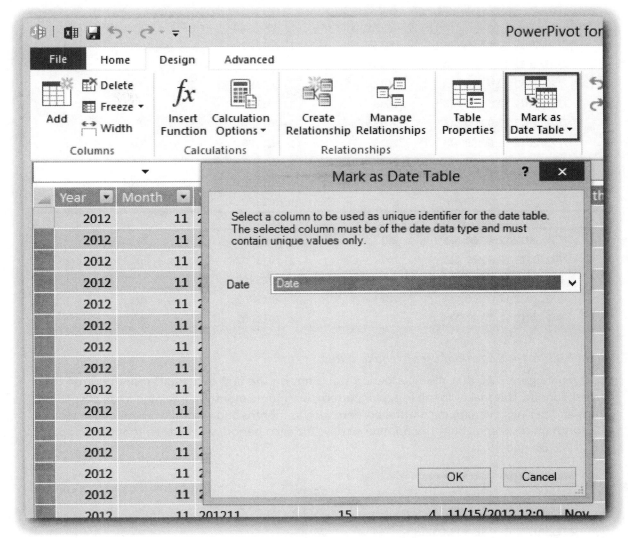

*Figure 3.41: You need to mark a column in the date table as DateTable in order for time intelligence functions to work.*

Jim has now prepared his model to use time intelligence functions.

### Power Pivot Tip: Working with Special Calendars, Like 4-4-5

Instead of a normal calendar there are many special calendars that are used for certain reporting scenarios. A common custom calendar used for managing accounting periods is the 4–4–5 calendar. It is used in retail, manufacturing and parking industry. When you're working with special calendars like the 4-4-5 calendar, you cannot use the DAX time intelligence functions. The time intelligence functions need a real date column in order to traverse time. In a 4-4-5 calendar, the dates are not predictable. In this type of calendar, a year is divided into four quarters. Each quarter has 13 weeks, which are grouped into two 4-week "months" and one 5-week "month." Also, a period always ends on the same day of the week, which makes comparisons of weeks easy to do. Although you cannot use the built-in time intelligence functions with this type of calendar, you can still use Power Pivot and DAX to deal with such special calendars. Figure 3.42 shows an example of a 4-4-5 calendar offset against a traditional date.

| Date | FyYear | FyMonth | 445Period | 445Year | 445Month |
|------|--------|---------|-----------|---------|----------|
| 7/20/2012 12:00:00 AM | 2013 | 1 | 2013P01 | 2013 | 1 |
| 7/21/2012 12:00:00 AM | 2013 | 1 | 2013P01 | 2013 | 1 |
| 7/22/2012 12:00:00 AM | 2013 | 1 | 2013P01 | 2013 | 1 |
| 7/23/2012 12:00:00 AM | 2013 | 1 | 2013P01 | 2013 | 1 |
| 7/24/2012 12:00:00 AM | 2013 | 1 | 2013P01 | 2013 | 1 |
| 7/25/2012 12:00:00 AM | 2013 | 1 | 2013P01 | 2013 | 1 |
| 7/26/2012 12:00:00 AM | 2013 | 1 | 2013P01 | 2013 | 1 |
| 7/27/2012 12:00:00 AM | 2013 | 1 | 2013P01 | 2013 | 1 |
| 7/28/2012 12:00:00 AM | 2013 | 1 | 2013P01 | 2013 | 1 |
| 7/29/2012 12:00:00 AM | 2013 | 1 | 2013P02 | 2013 | 2 |
| 7/30/2012 12:00:00 AM | 2013 | 1 | 2013P02 | 2013 | 2 |
| 7/31/2012 12:00:00 AM | 2013 | 1 | 2013P02 | 2013 | 2 |
| 8/1/2012 12:00:00 AM | 2013 | 2 | 2013P02 | 2013 | 2 |
| 8/2/2012 12:00:00 AM | 2013 | 2 | 2013P02 | 2013 | 2 |
| 8/3/2012 12:00:00 AM | 2013 | 2 | 2013P02 | 2013 | 2 |

*Figure 3.42: A 4-4-5 calendar uses irregular dates.*

Observe in Figure 3.42 that the new period starts not on the first of a "real" month but on the nearest Sunday. This makes for an irregular pattern, with some months containing more days than others and periods overlapping natural borders such as months and years. If you put 445Year and 445Month on rows and count the number of days for each period, you can see that there is pattern of 28, 28, and 35 days.

| | | |
|------|-----------|-----|
| 2012P05 | $1,416,310.91 | 28 |
| 2012P06 | $1,468,206.93 | 35 |
| 2012P07 | $1,403,052.35 | 28 |
| 2012P08 | $1,388,320.78 | 28 |
| 2012P09 | $1,376,213.66 | 35 |
| 2012P10 | $1,364,031.14 | 28 |
| 2012P11 | $1,354,621.97 | 28 |
| 2012P12 | $1,344,082.27 | 35 |
| Grand Total | $33,673,505.17 | 728 |

*Figure 3.43: Days per period in a 4-4-5 calendar period.*

So how do you work with this? Obviously, you can't rely on the "real" dates, so you need to work with some other mechanism. Also, there are some things that don't make much sense—like comparing previous periods—because the numbers of days don't really match up. Comparing year over year does make sense, though, because the same pattern repeats every year.

Let's look at two examples: how to get the same period last year and how to do a year-to-date (YTD) sum in a 4-4-5 calendar.

In order to be able to work with this special calendar, you need to make sure you have a numeric value for each period to work with. In the figures above, you see 445Year and 445Month columns that are numeric values you can work with.

The first calculated field to add is where to get the revenue for the same period last year:

```
[Sum of Revenue Previous Whole Year]=
    IF(HASONEVALUE(DateTable[445Year])
        ,CALCULATE([Sum of Revenue]
            ,ALL(DateTable)
            ,DateTable[445Year] =
                VALUES(DateTable[445Year])-1
        )
    )
```

In this calculated field, you check whether a single 445Year is selected (HASONEVALUE), and if it is, you calculate [Sum of Revenue] where DateTable[445Year] equals the value of DateTable[445Year] in the current PivotTable selection minus 1; you ignore any other filters on the date table by using the ALL function. This function doesn't use the actual date column to traverse in time, but it uses the column that came in from the data source.

Adding this calculated field to the PivotTable gives you the result you are looking for, as shown in Figure 3.44.

| Row Labels | Sum of Revenue | Sum of Revenue Previous Whole Year |
|---|---|---|
| 2011 | $18,242,884.44 | $11,134,865.36 |
| 2011P01 | | $11,134,865.36 |
| 2011P02 | $1,563,062.54 | $11,134,865.36 |
| 2011P03 | $3,091,815.97 | $11,134,865.36 |
| 2011P04 | | $11,134,865.36 |
| 2011P05 | $1,528,032.60 | $11,134,865.36 |
| 2011P06 | $3,142,207.45 | $11,134,865.36 |
| 2011P07 | | $11,134,865.36 |
| 2011P08 | $1,505,372.79 | $11,134,865.36 |
| 2011P09 | $2,961,899.78 | $11,134,865.36 |
| 2011P10 | | $11,134,865.36 |
| 2011P11 | $1,501,453.80 | $11,134,865.36 |
| 2011P12 | $2,949,039.52 | $11,134,865.36 |
| 2012 | $15,430,620.73 | $18,242,884.44 |
| 2012P01 | | $18,242,884.44 |
| 2012P02 | $1,450,147.99 | $18,242,884.44 |
| 2012P03 | $2,865,632.74 | $18,242,884.44 |
| 2012P04 | | $18,242,884.44 |
| 2012P05 | $1,416,310.91 | $18,242,884.44 |
| 2012P06 | $1,468,206.93 | $18,242,884.44 |
| 2012P07 | $1,403,052.35 | $18,242,884.44 |
| 2012P08 | $1,388,320.78 | $18,242,884.44 |
| 2012P09 | $1,376,213.66 | $18,242,884.44 |
| 2012P10 | $1,364,031.14 | $18,242,884.44 |
| 2012P11 | $1,354,621.97 | $18,242,884.44 |
| 2012P12 | $1,344,082.27 | $18,242,884.44 |
| Grand Total | $33,673,505.17 | |

Figure 3.44: Sum of revenue for the previous whole year in a 4-4-5 calendar.

Next, you need to calculate the same period last year. This calculated field is very similar to the one you just created:

```
[Sum of Revenue Same month previous year]=
    IF(HASONEVALUE(DateTable[445Year]) &&
        HASONEVALUE(DateTable[445Month]),
            CALCULATE([Sum of Revenue]
                ,ALL(DateTable)
                ,DateTable[445Year] =
                    values(DateTable[445Year])-1
                ,DateTable[445Month]=
                    values(DateTable[445Month])
            )
    )
```

In this case, you want to check for both 445Year and 445Month to be selected. Based on that, you want to go to the previous 445Year but still filter the 445Month with the same value. This will give you the same month last year.

| | Row Labels | Sum of Revenue | Sum of Revenue Same month previous year |
|---|---|---|---|
| 1 | Row Labels | Sum of Revenue | Sum of Revenue Same month previous year |
| 2 | ⊟2011 | $18,242,884.44 | |
| 3 | 2011P02 | $1,563,062.54 | |
| 4 | 2011P03 | $3,091,815.97 | |
| 5 | 2011P05 | $1,528,032.60 | |
| 6 | 2011P06 | $3,142,207.45 | $1,632,557.19 |
| 7 | 2011P08 | $1,505,372.79 | $1,619,680.27 |
| 8 | 2011P09 | $2,961,899.78 | $3,135,815.82 |
| 9 | 2011P10 | | $1,592,000.22 |
| 10 | 2011P11 | $1,501,453.80 | |
| 11 | 2011P12 | $2,949,039.52 | $3,154,811.86 |
| 12 | ⊟2012 | $15,430,620.73 | |
| 13 | 2012P02 | $1,450,147.99 | $1,563,062.54 |
| 14 | 2012P03 | $2,865,632.74 | $3,091,815.97 |
| 15 | 2012P05 | $1,416,310.91 | $1,528,032.60 |
| 16 | 2012P06 | $1,468,206.93 | $3,142,207.45 |
| 17 | 2012P07 | $1,403,052.35 | |
| 18 | 2012P08 | $1,388,320.78 | $1,505,372.79 |
| 19 | 2012P09 | $1,376,213.66 | $2,961,899.78 |
| 20 | 2012P10 | $1,364,031.14 | |
| 21 | 2012P11 | $1,354,621.97 | $1,501,453.80 |
| 22 | 2012P12 | $1,344,082.27 | $2,949,039.52 |
| 23 | Grand Total | $33,673,505.17 | |

*Figure 3.45: Revenue in the same month of the previous year for a 445 period.*

Now, in a final calculated field, you use HASONEVALUE to combine the two calculated fields to allow the user to use a single calculated field that will do the right thing, based on what is shown in the PivotTable:

```
[Sum of Revenue previous year 445]=
    IF(HASONEVALUE(DateTable[445Period])
        ,[Sum of Revenue Same month previous year]
        ,IF(HASONEVALUE(DateTable[445Year])
            ,[Sum of Revenue Previous Whole Year])
    )
```

Putting this calculated field in the PivotTable will give you a result that compares the revenue per 4-4-5 period with last year for both entire years or periods.

| Row Labels ⊤ | Sum of Revenue | Sum of Revenue previous year 445 |
|---|---|---|
| ⊟ 2011 | $18,242,884.44 | $11,134,865.36 |
| 2011P02 | $1,563,062.54 | |
| 2011P03 | $3,091,815.97 | |
| 2011P05 | $1,528,032.60 | |
| 2011P06 | $3,142,207.45 | $1,632,557.19 |
| 2011P08 | $1,505,372.79 | $1,619,680.27 |
| 2011P09 | $2,961,899.78 | $3,135,815.82 |
| 2011P11 | $1,501,453.80 | $1,592,000.22 |
| 2011P12 | $2,949,039.52 | $3,154,811.86 |
| ⊟ 2012 | $15,430,620.73 | $18,242,884.44 |
| 2012P02 | $1,450,147.99 | $1,563,062.54 |
| 2012P03 | $2,865,632.74 | $3,091,815.97 |
| 2012P05 | $1,416,310.91 | $1,528,032.60 |
| 2012P06 | $1,468,206.93 | $1,628,475.46 |
| 2012P07 | $1,403,052.35 | $1,513,731.99 |
| 2012P08 | $1,388,320.78 | $1,505,372.79 |
| 2012P09 | $1,376,213.66 | $1,491,404.76 |
| 2012P10 | $1,364,031.14 | $1,470,495.02 |
| 2012P11 | $1,354,621.97 | $1,501,453.80 |
| 2012P12 | $1,344,082.27 | $1,490,817.05 |
| Grand Total | $33,673,505.17 | |

Figure 3.46: Comparing revenue over years with a 4-4-5 calendar.

Another interesting calculation is determining the YTD sum of revenue for the 4-4-5 calendar:

```
[Sum of Revenue 445 YTD]=
    IF(HASONEVALUE(DateTable[445Year])
        && HASONEVALUE(DateTable[445Month])
            ,CALCULATE([Sum of Revenue]
                    ,ALL(DateTable)
                    ,DateTable[445Year] =
                     VALUES (DateTable[445Year])
                    ,DateTable[445Month] <=
                     VALUES(DateTable[445Month])
                    )
        ,[Sum of Revenue]
    )
```

This calculated field is another variation on the same theme as before. However, in this case, you want to keep the filter for the current year but calculate the revenue for all the months leading up to and including the current month used in the PivotTable. Adding this to the PivotTable gives you the YTD calculation for the 4-4-5 calendar.

| Row Labels ▼ | Sum of Revenue | Sum of Revenue previous year 445 | Sum of Revenue 445 YTD |
|---|---|---|---|
| ⊟ 2011 | $18,242,884.44 | $11,134,865.36 | $18,242,884.44 |
| 2011P02 | $1,563,062.54 | | $1,563,062.54 |
| 2011P03 | $3,091,815.97 | | $4,654,878.51 |
| 2011P04 | | | $4,654,878.51 |
| 2011P05 | $1,528,032.60 | | $6,182,911.10 |
| 2011P06 | $3,142,207.45 | $1,632,557.19 | $9,325,118.55 |
| 2011P07 | | | $9,325,118.55 |
| 2011P08 | $1,505,372.79 | $1,619,680.27 | $10,830,491.34 |
| 2011P09 | $2,961,899.78 | $3,135,815.82 | $13,792,391.12 |
| 2011P10 | | $1,592,000.22 | $13,792,391.12 |
| 2011P11 | $1,501,453.80 | | $15,293,844.92 |
| 2011P12 | $2,949,039.52 | $3,154,811.86 | $18,242,884.44 |
| ⊟ 2012 | $15,430,620.73 | $18,242,884.44 | $15,430,620.73 |
| 2012P02 | $1,450,147.99 | $1,563,062.54 | $1,450,147.99 |
| 2012P03 | $2,865,632.74 | $3,091,815.97 | $4,315,780.73 |
| 2012P04 | | | $4,315,780.73 |
| 2012P05 | $1,416,310.91 | $1,528,032.60 | $5,732,091.64 |
| 2012P06 | $1,468,206.93 | $3,142,207.45 | $7,200,298.57 |
| 2012P07 | $1,403,052.35 | | $8,603,350.91 |
| 2012P08 | $1,388,320.78 | $1,505,372.79 | $9,991,671.70 |
| 2012P09 | $1,376,213.66 | $2,961,899.78 | $11,367,885.35 |
| 2012P10 | $1,364,031.14 | | $12,731,916.50 |
| 2012P11 | $1,354,621.97 | $1,501,453.80 | $14,086,538.47 |
| 2012P12 | $1,344,082.27 | $2,949,039.52 | $15,430,620.73 |
| Grand Total | $33,673,505.17 | | $33,673,505.17 |

*Figure 3.47: YTD calculation using a 4-4-5 calendar.*

As you can see, you don't have to use the built-in time intelligence functions to work with calendars and dates. Using those functions does make life easier when you can use them, though. Of course, there might be some special calendars that require different approaches. Descriptions of some other approaches can be found in blog posts by Rob Collie (http://ppivot.us/qahr6) and Marco Russo (http://ppivot.us/eKcKI).

# Reporting over the Past 12 Months

Jim needs to report over the past 12 months. Instead of solving this problem by using a calculation, Jim decides to add another calculated column to the DateTable table that he can use as a filter on his PivotTables:

```
[Running 12 months]=
    IF(
        [Date] >= EOMONTH(
                [Absolute Last Invoice Date],-12
        )+1
    &&
        [Date] < =EOMONTH(
        [Absolute Last Invoice Date],0
        )
    ,1
    ,0)
```

This calculated column returns 1 when the date value is between the first day of the month 12 months before the last invoice date and the end of the month of the last invoice date.

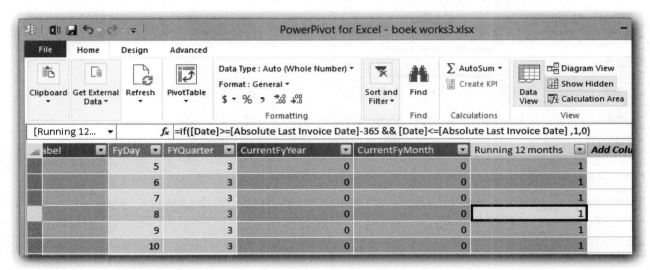

*Figure 3.48: The formulas in the calculated column will be evaluated every time the data is refreshed.*

Jim will now be able to use these calculated columns in his reports to make his life a little easier.

## Updating the Data

During the two days that Jim was working on preparing the model, new data became available, and Jim needs this new data in his dashboard. Power Pivot has the ability to load new data with ease. Jim can simply click Refresh in the Power Pivot tab to get two options: Refresh the Current Table and Refresh the Data for All

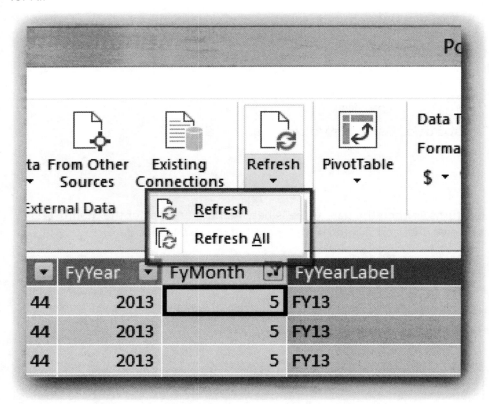

*Figure 3.49: Refresh a single table or all the tables in the Model.*

Refreshing the data also causes the calculated columns to recalculate. So, for example, when new invoices with later dates are loaded into the model, CurrentFyMonth might then return different values.

Jim has now prepared his model, and he is ready to start doing analytics and create his dashboard.

# 4- Building a Dashboard in Excel

In this chapter Jim creates the dashboard in Excel using the Excel Data Model he set up in the previous chapter. Jim creates various data visualizations needed for his dashboard by using native Excel features like PivotTables, PivotCharts and Sparklines and uses Power Pivot DAX formulas to get the values he needs.

## Getting Set Up in Excel

Now that Jim has prepared the layout of his model, he starts building the dashboard and reports. To get started, Jim uses an Excel best practice and creates a worksheet that contains just raw data that can be used in the reports and dashboard but hides this worksheet so it's not visible to the user.

Jim knows he needs to collect some basic information to display on the dashboard, and to determine what to collect, he answers questions like these:

- What is the last date for which we have data that is used in the report? How fresh is the data?
- What are the current year and month we are reporting on?

The workbook right now has one worksheet with data used to validate the last fiscal date measure. Jim adds a new worksheet and renames it from Sheet2 to DataSheet. He then deletes Sheet1 because he doesn't need it anymore.

Jim wants to show the last invoice date, which will help him display the last date for which there is data in the report. To do this, he adds a new calculated field to the model that looks very much like the [Absolute Last Invoice Date] calculated field (see Chapter 3). He selects Power Pivot, Calculated Fields, New Calculated Field.

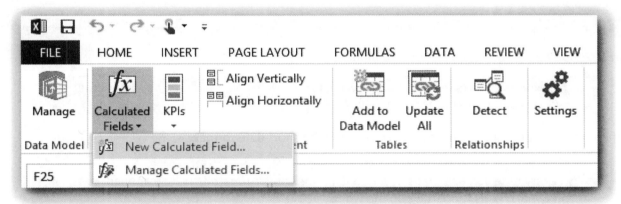

*Figure 4.1: Adding a calculated field to the Power Pivot data model.*

The Calculated Field dialog that appears allows Jim to add an expression to the Power Pivot model. Jim adds the following expression:

```
[Absolute Last Invoice Date] =
CALCULATE(LASTDATE(Invoice[Date])
        ,ALL(Invoice)
        )
```

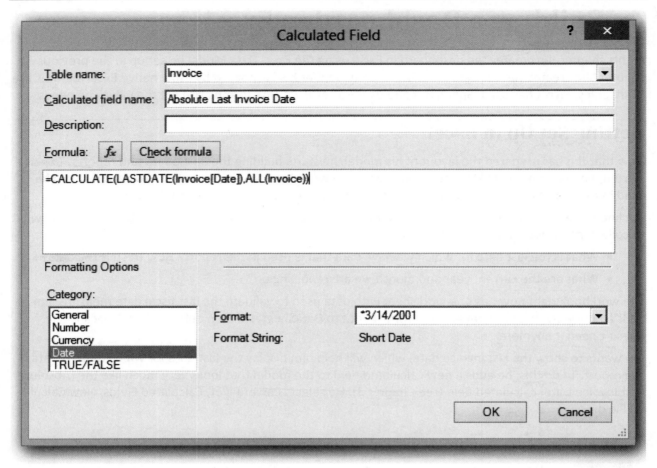

*Figure 4.2: Adding an expression to the data model.*

> This expression gets the LASTDATE value for the Date column for all the rows of the
> Invoice table, thanks to the ALL(Invoice) argument.

Jim then sets Format String to Short Date by selecting the short date format.

> When you set the formatting in a calculated field, the field will store that formatting,
> so every time you use that calculated field, the same formatting will be applied. You
> can overrule this formatting on the worksheet.

Now Jim goes back to the DataSheet worksheet and creates a PivotTable. In the Fields area, he adds FyYear
and FyMonth under Rows, CurrentFyMonth under Filters (with the value 1 selected), and Absolute Last
Invoice Date under Values. This PivotTable provides three values Jim can use in his report.

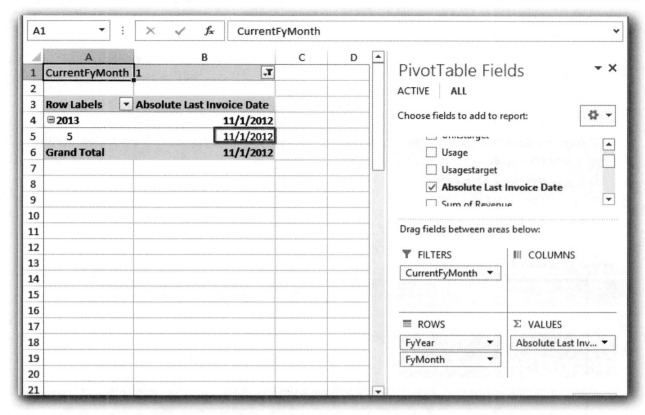

*Figure 4.3: Creating a PivotTable to get the latest date.*

Jim notices that reports in his company usually have a clear distinction between fiscal and calendar dates. He therefore decides to add two calculated column that add a fiscal year label to his model. He opens the Power Pivot window, selects the DateTable table, and inserts the columns next to the FyMonth column by right-clicking the column and selecting Insert Column.

| WeekNumber | FyYear | FyMonth | FyYearLabel | FyMo |
|---|---|---|---|---|
| 44 | 2013 | | Create Relationship... | 5 |
| 44 | 2013 | | Navigate to Related Table | 5 |
| 44 | 2013 | | Copy | 5 |
| 45 | 2013 | | Insert Column | 5 |
| 45 | 2013 | | Delete Columns | 5 |
| 45 | 2013 | | Rename Column | 5 |
| 45 | 2013 | | Freeze Columns | 5 |
| 45 | 2013 | | Unfreeze All Columns | 5 |
| 45 | 2013 | | Hide from Client Tools | 5 |
| 45 | 2013 | | Column Width... | 5 |
| 46 | 2013 | | Filter ▶ | 5 |
| 46 | 2013 | | Description... | 5 |

*Figure 4.4: Inserting a calculated column between two columns in Power Pivot.*

Jim uses the following three DAX formulas to get the correct labels:

```
[FyYearLabel]=
  "FY" & RIGHT([FyYear],2)
```

This formula adds the text FY before the last two characters of the FyYear column.

```
[FyMonthLabel]=
  "M" & FORMAT([FyMonth],"00")
```

This formula adds the text M before the FyMonth column and adds a trailing 0 when the month is only one character.

```
[FyQuarterLabel]=
  "Q"&[FYQuarter]
```

This formula adds the text Q before the value of the FyQuarter column.

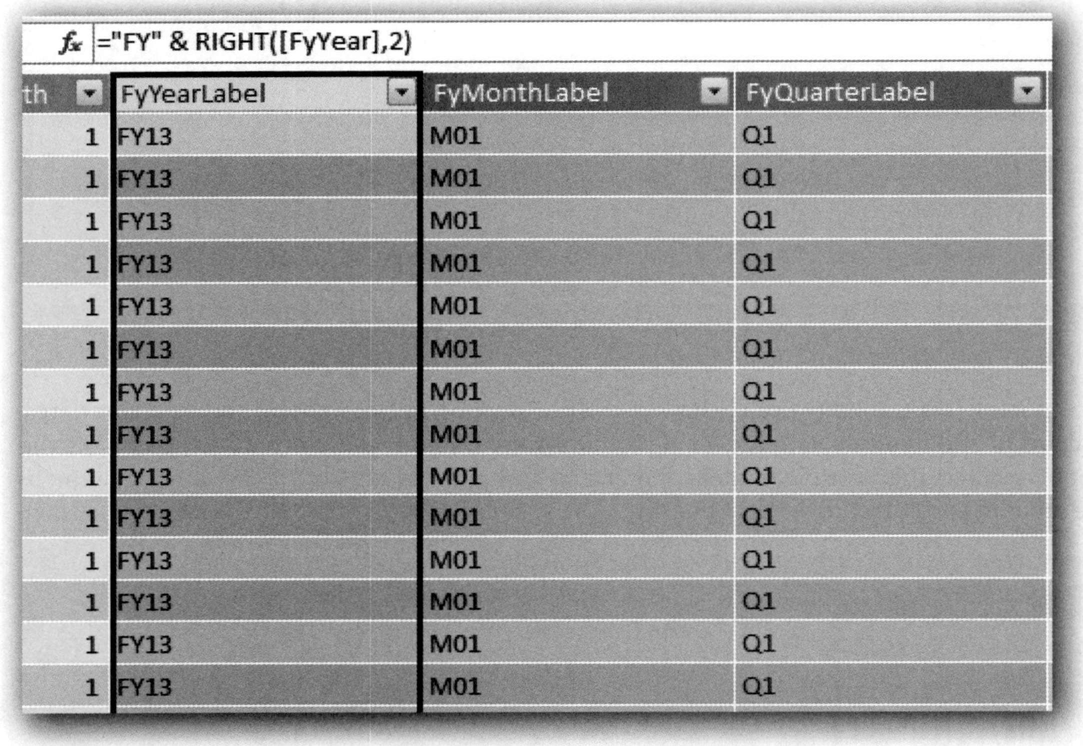

| $f_x$ | ="FY" & RIGHT([FyYear],2) | | |
|---|---|---|---|
| th ▾ | FyYearLabel ▾ | FyMonthLabel ▾ | FyQuarterLabel ▾ |
| 1 | FY13 | M01 | Q1 |
| 1 | FY13 | M01 | Q1 |
| 1 | FY13 | M01 | Q1 |
| 1 | FY13 | M01 | Q1 |
| 1 | FY13 | M01 | Q1 |
| 1 | FY13 | M01 | Q1 |
| 1 | FY13 | M01 | Q1 |
| 1 | FY13 | M01 | Q1 |
| 1 | FY13 | M01 | Q1 |
| 1 | FY13 | M01 | Q1 |
| 1 | FY13 | M01 | Q1 |
| 1 | FY13 | M01 | Q1 |
| 1 | FY13 | M01 | Q1 |
| 1 | FY13 | M01 | Q1 |

*Figure 4.5: Three calculated columns added to Power Pivot.*

When Jim now swaps out the FyYear and FyMonth columns for the new FyYearLabel and FyMonthLabel, he sees the updated terminology used in the PivotTable.

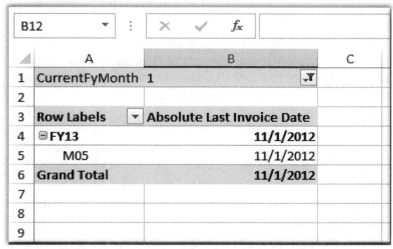

*Figure 4.6: Fiscal year labels added to the PivotTable.*

# Creating the Dashboard

Jim has prepared his model to the point that he can now start creating the actual dashboard. Before Jim goes any further in actually creating the dashboard, he needs to plan it.

## Taking Inventory and Planning the Dashboard

The goal of the dashboard is to help the management team get quick insights in the requests they make, so Jim creates a list of all requests the board made and then prioritizes the list as follows:

1. What is the rhythm of the business? How are our key metrics doing?

2. Did the revenue pick up for all regions?

3. Did the new PR effort have an effect in the new markets?

4. What are our top products? Are they improving?

5. Did the cost reduction effort pan out as expected?

### Dashboard Tip: Choosing the Right Information

One of the most important principles in creating a dashboard is that it should present information so that it's understandable and can be read in a short amount of time. You need to make tough decisions about what information to include in a dashboard and what not to include. You have a limited amount of space on a dashboard. Besides talking in person to the dashboard users, it is often a good idea to look at the company's business plan or annual report. These reports usually outline the short-term (next year) and long-term plans, intended initiatives, and goals. These items are usually top of mind in most board rooms and allow great insights into what the business finds interesting (and what it doesn't).

Jim has made some decisions based on his interviews with management. One of the most important lessons he has learned over time is to iterate often with the "customer"—in this case, the CFO. He often sends out quick emails to the CFO for feedback to make sure his decisions work for her.

### Dashboard Tip: Doing Short Iterations and Getting Feedback Often

As a dashboard is progressing, make sure you get feedback from those who will use the dashboard. Show them what you have and ask them for their input. In the end, they have to use it, and it's your job to make sure the information is conveyed appropriately. It's better to get negative feedback early than later on, after you've done a lot of work. Also, by including the users in the design process, you make them part of the design, and they will embrace the end result even more because they contributed to it.

# Setting Up the Dashboard

Jim now adds a new worksheet to the Excel workbook and calls it DashBoard. On every Excel sheet that Jim uses to create reports, he keeps two vertical rows and one horizontal row empty. He uses one horizontal row and one vertical row to create spacing between the report and the border. He uses the other vertical row to hide the Excel selection grid active cell selection when he publishes the report.

### Dashboard Tip: No Scrolling!

The information on a dashboard has to be readable at a glance. If users need to scroll to see data, they won't be able to see it immediately. Users often don't bother to look outside the immediate screen, so contain your dashboard to one screen that the user can easily take in all at once.

Next, Jim adds the title of the dashboard (Strategic Targets Dashboard) and two important labels to show when the data was refreshed last and what the current reporting period is. He chooses a light text color and adds a thick line under the title bar.

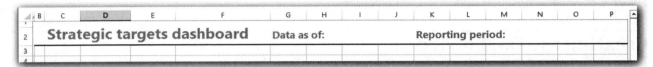

*Figure 4.7: Adding the title bar and two labels to the dashboard.*

### Dashboard Tip: Choosing the Right Colors for Your Dashboard

It is important to spend time thinking about the colors you want to use in a dashboard. Colors can be grouped into two types: aggressive and passive. The aggressive colors (such as red and green) attract attention immediately and imply importance, while the passive colors (such as light gray) are soothing to the eye.

You don't want to attract attention to anything in your dashboard that doesn't warrant it. For example, using big bright labels with all uppercase and bold font will attract the eyes away from the actual data presented.

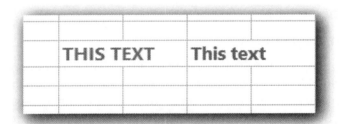

*Figure 4.8: The brighter, all-uppercase label attracts the eye immediately.*

Contextual data such as labels should never compete with the actual data on the dashboard. Such labels provide additional information that a user needs only when learning what data the dashboard displays.

If you use color to attract the user's attention, make sure to use it sparingly. Otherwise, the user will get used to it, and it will no longer be a differentiator.

Define a set of colors that you want to use for a dashboard up front and try to add a new color to the set only when needed.

Jim wants to use data he added to the DataSheet workbook to display the last date the data was refreshed. Jim selects the cell where he added the Data as Of label and types the following formula in the Excel formula bar:

```
="Data as of: " &
```

He then navigates to the DataSheet workbook and clicks the Absolute Last Invoice Date field on the Grand Total row of the PivotTable.

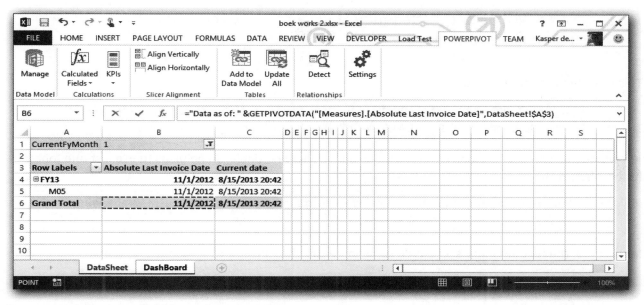

*Figure 4.9: Selecting a field from the PivotTable.*

By clicking the cell Excel adds the reference to the cell to the formula in Excel:

```
="Data as of: " &
 GETPIVOTDATA("[Measures].[Last Invoice Date]",
 DataSheet!$A$3)
```

### Excel Tip: The Excel `GETPIVOTDATA` Function

The formula that Excel uses here to get the values is not the normal cell reference but uses the Excel function `GETPIVOTDATA`. This function returns data from a PivotTable. Where you click in the PivotTable is important because the `GETPIVOTDATA` function uses the values from the rows and columns on the axis as a filter to get the right value. In this case, using the Grand Total row is important because it will make sure the user always gets a value returned, even when the fiscal month and year change over time. For more information, see http://ppivot.us/OWX5f.

The result is not what Jim expects.

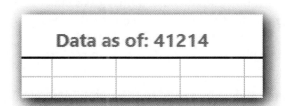

*Figure 4.10: Unexpected values in the label.*

From experience, Jim knows what has happened here: Excel stores dates as numeric values, and when you use the `GETPIVOTDATA` function, you need to tell Excel that you want to see the data as a date by formatting the output. Jim uses the Excel `TEXT` function to add formatting to the output of the `GETPIV-OTDATA` function. He changes the formula in Excel to:

```
="Data as of: " &
 TEXT(
  GETPIVOTDATA( "[Measures].[Last Invoice Date]",
  DataSheet!$A$3)
 ,"mm/dd/yyyy")
```

This gives Jim the output he expects.

> To learn more about dates and times in Excel, see Microsoft's "How to Use Dates and Times in Excel," at http://ppivot.us/BRNZW.

Jim wants to create a workbook that looks crisp and is easily readable, so he plans to use just one font for his dashboard: Segoe UI.

> For more tips and tricks on spreadsheet formatting, see this blog post from Power-PivotPro.com: http://ppivot.us/EEXJM.

In this case, the text Jim adds is a header, so he increases the font size to 14 and makes it bold.

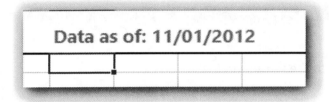

*Figure 4.11: A crisply formatted label.*

## Dashboard Tip: Using Fonts

The same principles you consider with colors apply to fonts as well. For example, using too many fonts will distract a user from the information that you want to display. Before you start working on a dashboard or report, decide what fonts to use and stick to a maximum of two fonts to reduce distraction.

While working on this book, I stumbled across research from MIT which found that a badly chosen font for a car dashboard can distract you from the road and increase your chance of crashing (see http://ppivot.us/SSFPC). This is a good lesson in how important typography can be.

Another factor that might be important is that a dashboard may need to use a business's standard typography and colors. Does the company have a default font? Maybe even colors? The CFO and CIO usually spend many dollars on the website or corporate style and usually like it if they see these settings used in company reports as well. It's usually easy to find the company colors, typography and styling by looking at a company's website.

Jim wants to make sure the rest of his dashboard keeps the same styling he's used to this point. Maintaining the same styling in the entire report is pretty labor intensive, though, so he decides to spend a little energy setting up a style that he can easily reuse. He selects a cell that has the styling he wants to apply everywhere and clicks Home, Styles, More, New Cell Style.

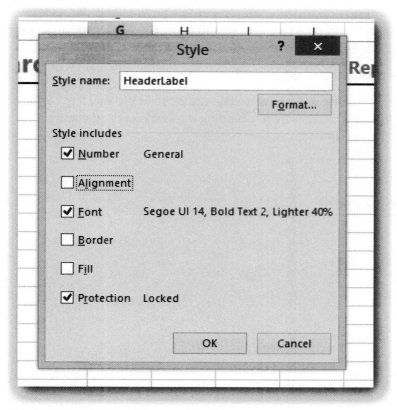

*Figure 4.12: Creating a new cell style.*

In the Style dialog that appears, Jim names the style HeaderLabel and deselects Alignment, Border, and Fill since he doesn't want to apply those characteristics generally.

Most text in the report will not be header text, so Jim also creates a DashboardText style that is set to 10-point Segoe UI font. He will now be able to quickly apply styles across his dashboard by simply selecting them from the style gallery.

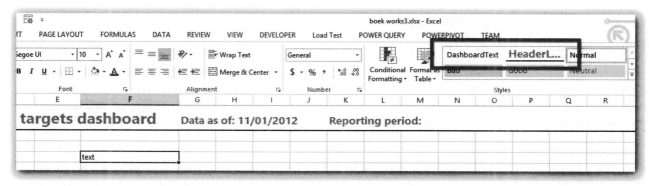

*Figure 4.13: The style gallery.*

## Calculating Year-over-Year Change and Variance to Target by Region

Jim is now ready to add the first piece of data to the dashboard. In one of the interview sessions, he learned that revenue isn't equal for all regions. It is very important for the management team to keep an eye on the revenue by region. Therefore, Jim adds to the dashboard the revenue, the revenue variance to target, the year-over-year change for the current month, and the variance-to-target trend over time by region for the current month.

The company uses several acronyms in its reports: $VTT stands for variance to target in dollars, and YoY% means year-over-year change in percentage. Jim will use these in the dashboards and reports.

Jim creates a PivotTable in the DashBoard worksheet by opening the Power Pivot add-in and selects Home. Then he opens the Power Pivot add-in and selects Home, PivotTable to add a PivotTable to the worksheet. Jim selects the cell C4 on the DashBoard worksheet for positioning the PivotTable.

### Dashboard Tip: Keeping space around the edges

By using the first row and column of a worksheet you put your data too close to the row and column headers and the report looks to dense and busy. By not keeping the first rows and columns empty it will become very hard to do this at a later stage.

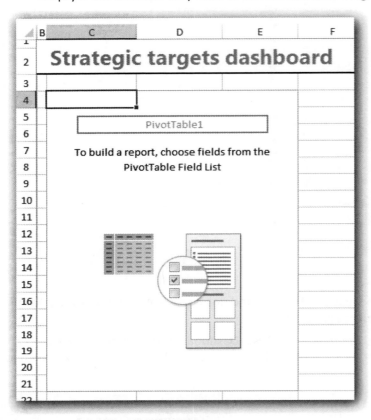

*Figure 4.14: Inserting a PivotTable.*

Jim now adds the Region field from the PoliticalGeography table to Rows on the PivotTable, and he adds RevenueAmount and RevenueTarget from the Invoice table under Values. The columns that are dragged in the Values area are automatically aggregated for each region; in this case, they are aggregated using SUM. Power Pivot automatically creates two implicit calculated fields for Jim.

### Power Pivot Tip: Implicit Calculated Fields

Whenever you drag fields into a PivotTable to be aggregated, Excel or Power Pivot creates a calculated field under the covers, with a name that consists of the type of aggregation and the field name (for example, Sum of SalesAmount). Excel (in Excel 2013) or Power Pivot (in Excel 2010) creates these calculated fields in the data model implicitly—hence their name implicit calculated fields. You don't notice these calculated fields unless you try to create a calculated field with the same name.

Implicit calculated fields are great for data exploration. However, when you are building a real report or dashboard, the general best practice is to not use implicit calculated fields but instead create your own calculated fields. You can remove previously creates implicit calculated fields in the Power Pivot add-in by selecting Advanced, Show Implicit Calculated Fields and deleting these special fields. Deleting is the only option; you cannot modify implicit calculated fields. For more on implicit calculated fields, see page 34 in DAX Formulas for PowerPivot by Rob Collie (http://ppivot.us/gYukh), who is quite passionate about them and swears he never used them.

One of the primary values that Jim wants to display in the dashboard and reports is the sum of revenue. He creates a calculated field that he can control himself and that he can use as a base for other calculated fields. He creates a new calculated field by opening the Power Pivot window, selecting the RevenueAmount column in the Invoice table, and clicking AutoSum. Power Pivot creates a calculated field named Sum of RevenueAmount 2 as there already is an implicit calculated field called Sum of RevenueAmount. Jim re-names it Sum of Revenue.

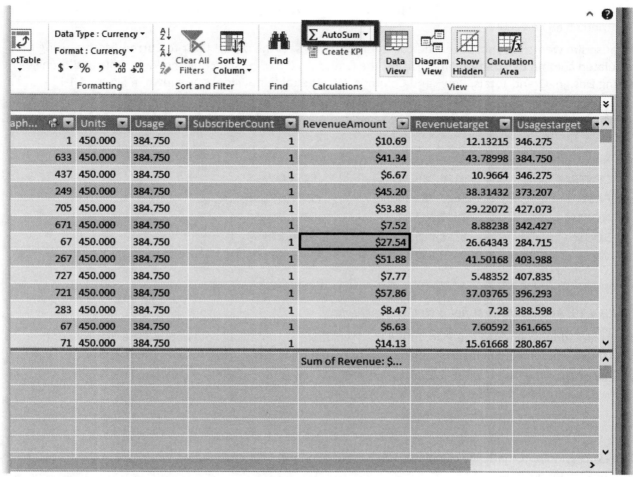

*Figure 4.15: Creating calculated fields in the calculation area.*

Jim now has the following calculated field:

        [Sum of Revenue] =
          SUM([RevenueAmount])

And he has this revenue target calculation:

        [Sum of RevenueTarget] =
          SUM([Revenuetarget])

For both of these calculated fields, Jim sets the format to currency.

## Power Pivot Tip: Creating and Managing Calculated Fields

As a Power Pivot model gets more complex and you add more business logic to it, it becomes more and more important that you manage your calculated fields. Here are a few tips that will help you manage large models with complex calculated fields:

• Split a complex calculated field into several separate calculated fields. This allows you to create and debug parts of the calculation separately. You might also be able to reuse calculated fields, which makes mistakes less likely.

- Choose similar names for calculations over the same base field—for example, Sum of Revenue, Count of Revenue, Revenue YoY%, and Revenue to Target.

- Name a calculated field as clearly as possible to describe what it does.

- Hide calculated fields that are not directly used or useful in reports (for example, intermediate calculated fields).

- Format calculated fields appropriately to save work later and ensure that the numbers are perceived correctly.

Because Jim wants to report over the current month, he sets the report filter to CurrentMonth, using the calculated column he created. Jim turns off the Grand Total row by selecting the PivotTable and then selecting Design, Grand Totals, Rows and Columns, Off. The table now looks as shown in Figure 4.16.

| CurrentFyMonth 1 | | |
|---|---|---|
| Row Labels ▾ | Sum of Revenue | Sum of RevenueTarget |
| CENTRAL | $176,989.31 | $154,005.25 |
| EAST | $621,381.14 | $507,861.36 |
| NORTH | $437,551.91 | $391,540.54 |
| SOUTH | $178,088.65 | $136,230.04 |
| WEST | $426,652.55 | $349,042.04 |

*Figure 4.16: Adding the first fields to the PivotTable.*

When Jim added a filter to the PivotTable, the PivotTable automatically overlapped the first row of the worksheet. Therefore, Jim inserts a blank row between rows 1 and 2 to preserve the space.

Instead of showing the revenue and its target directly, Jim wants to show the variance to target, so he adds a new calculated field with the following expression:

```
[Revenue to target]=
    [Sum of Revenue] - [Sum of Revenuetarget]
```

This expression automatically calculates the variance to target for each region when put in the PivotTable, with Region under Rows.

Next, Jim changes the Formatting Options Category setting to Currency and indicates that the calculated field should reside in the Invoice table.

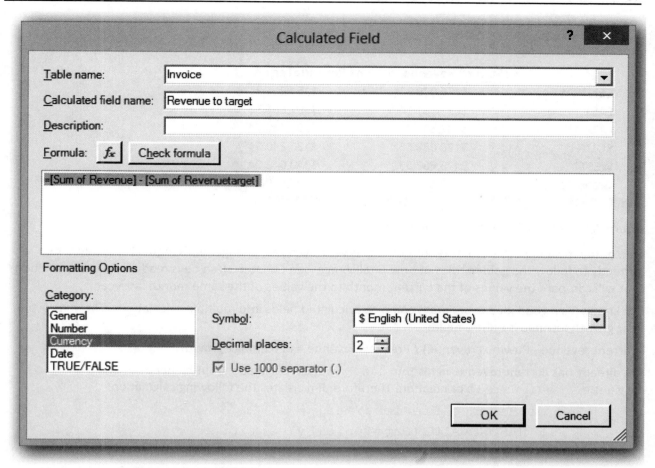

*Figure 4.17: Creating a calculated field.*

Adding a new calculated field to the data model while selecting a PivotTable automatically adds the calculated field to the PivotTable.

| CurrentFyMonth 1 | | | |
| --- | --- | --- | --- |
| Row Labels | Sum of Revenue | Sum of Revenuetarget | Revenue to target |
| CENTRAL | $176,989.31 | $154,039.00 | $22,950.31 |
| EAST | $621,381.14 | $507,939.00 | $113,442.14 |
| NORTH | $437,551.91 | $391,537.00 | $46,014.91 |
| SOUTH | $178,088.65 | $136,228.00 | $41,860.65 |
| WEST | $426,652.55 | $349,008.00 | $77,644.55 |
| Grand Total | $1,840,663.56 | $1,538,751.00 | $301,912.56 |

*Figure 4.18: A calculated field added to a PivotTable.*

Now Jim can remove the Sum of RevenueTarget column from the PivotTable.

Next, Jim wants to add some styling. To apply 10-point Segoe UI font to the PivotTable, he selects the text and clicks the "DashboardText" style from the style gallery on the home tab. Next he wants to change the style of the PivotTable to a clean and tidy look, he clicks on PivotTable tab, Design and selects the None style from the PivotTable style gallery. He makes the column headers bold and removes all the borders in the table, and then he reapplies a single bottom border to the column header. Jim also removes the Row Labels text and removes the Grand Total row.

| CurrentFyMonth | 1 | ⫧ | |
| --- | --- | --- | --- |
|  | **Sum of Revenue** | **Sum of RevenueTarget** | |
| CENTRAL | $176,989.31 | $154,005.25 |
| EAST | $621,381.14 | $507,861.36 |
| NORTH | $437,551.91 | $391,540.54 |
| SOUTH | $178,088.65 | $136,230.04 |
| WEST | $426,652.55 | $349,042.04 |
| Grand Total | $1,840,663.56 | $1,538,679.23 |

*Figure 4.19: Formatting applied to the PivotTable.*

One of the most important metrics for Contoso is year-over-year change. Jim's model is already set up correctly to follow the golden rules of time intelligence (see Chapter 3), so he is ready to create a function that will compare the values of the current month to the values of the same month last year.

Jim knows it's a good idea to separate complex calculated fields into multiple calculations. The year-over-year growth formula is quite simple:

(Current revenue - Previous revenue) / Previous revenue = Percentage growth

Jim already has current revenue in his `Sum of Revenue` calculation, but he needs to add a `Sum of Revenue PreviousYear` calculation. Therefore, Jim creates the following calculation:

```
[Sum of Revenue PreviousYear] =
    IF(HASONEVALUE(DateTable[FyYear]),
        CALCULATE([Sum of Revenue]
                                ,DATEADD(DateTable[Date]
                                ,-1
                                ,YEAR
                                )
            )
        )
```

This calculation determines `[Sum of Revenue]` for the dates in the current cell of the PivotTable and uses the `DATEADD` function to move those dates back one year in time, based on the values of the DateTable table. Jim wants to make sure that when this calculation is used in other reports, it won't throw an error when DAX is unable to find the right dates. He therefore uses the `HASONEVALUE` function to check whether the current cell contains only one value returned for the `DateTable[FyYear]` column. The `else` argument of the `IF` functions is optional; when it is omitted, DAX automatically returns `BLANK`.

## Power Pivot Tip: Understanding How Time Intelligence Functions Work

What does it mean that the calculation above will calculate the sum of revenue shifted backward in time by one year from the dates in the current context?

When you use time intelligence functions like `DATEADD` and `SAMEPERIODLASTYEAR`, DAX tries to determine the dates in the current period selected in the current cell. The following example shows the sum of revenue by fiscal year (in the boxes) and by fiscal month (underlined).

| | A | B |
|---|---|---|
| 1 | | |
| 2 | | |
| 3 | Row Labels ▼ | Sum of Revenue |
| 4 | ⊟ FY12 | $19,436,488.51 |
| 5 | M01 | $1,609,312.88 |
| 6 | M02 | $1,648,915.76 |
| 7 | M03 | $1,781,446.87 |
| 8 | M04 | $1,705,202.55 |
| 9 | M05 | $1,623,453.75 |
| 10 | M06 | $1,756,153.29 |
| 11 | M07 | $1,550,087.81 |
| 12 | M08 | $1,468,985.39 |
| 13 | M09 | $1,463,013.24 |
| 14 | M10 | $1,568,567.87 |
| 15 | M11 | $1,596,141.88 |
| 16 | M12 | $1,665,207.22 |
| 17 | ⊟ FY13 | $8,770,807.12 |
| 18 | M01 | $1,706,178.98 |
| 19 | M02 | $1,669,749.41 |
| 20 | M03 | $1,736,790.86 |
| 21 | M04 | $1,817,424.32 |
| 22 | M05 | $1,840,663.56 |
| 23 | Grand Total | $28,207,295.63 |

*Figure 4.20: Showing the PivotTable context.*

DAX tries to use the dates in the DateTable table that are set up using the time intelligence golden rules to determine what period is selected in the range for the current cell. It recognizes the boxed values to be by year and the underlined ones to be by month. DAX is able to recognize years, quarters, months, and days. It uses the start and end dates for that entire period in the DateTable table to traverse backward or forward in time; it does not use the actual dates that you have as values. In this example, notice that 2013 has data for only five months' worth of data, but this does not mean that DAX will use only those five months when getting the data for the previous year; it will use the entire year because for the year selection, the entire period is selected. In 2013, the last seven months don't have data, so they won't be shown on a month level.

Figure 4.21 shows what happens when you add the previous year formula to the PivotTable.

| | Row Labels ▼ | Sum of Revenue | Sum of Revenue PreviousYear |
|---|---|---|---|
| 3 | | | |
| 4 | ⊟ FY12 | **$19,436,488.51** | $19,370,393.94 |
| 5 | M01 | $1,609,312.88 | $1,706,391.03 |
| 6 | M02 | $1,648,915.76 | $1,696,727.20 |
| 7 | M03 | $1,781,446.87 | $1,690,528.11 |
| 8 | M04 | $1,705,202.55 | $1,676,105.52 |
| 9 | M05 | $1,623,453.75 | $1,664,064.20 |
| 10 | M06 | $1,756,153.29 | $1,772,804.54 |
| 11 | M07 | $1,550,087.81 | $1,638,170.46 |
| 12 | M08 | $1,468,985.39 | $1,626,721.29 |
| 13 | M09 | $1,463,013.24 | $1,382,612.06 |
| 14 | M10 | $1,568,567.87 | $1,290,114.19 |
| 15 | M11 | $1,596,141.88 | $1,615,586.60 |
| 16 | M12 | $1,665,207.22 | $1,610,568.74 |
| 17 | ⊟ FY13 | **$8,770,807.12** | **$19,436,488.51** |
| 18 | M01 | $1,706,178.98 | $1,609,312.88 |
| 19 | M02 | $1,669,749.41 | $1,648,915.76 |
| 20 | M03 | $1,736,790.86 | $1,781,446.87 |
| 21 | M04 | $1,817,424.32 | $1,705,202.55 |
| 22 | M05 | $1,840,663.56 | $1,623,453.75 |
| 23 | M06 | | $1,756,153.29 |
| 24 | M07 | | $1,550,087.81 |
| 25 | M08 | | $1,468,985.39 |
| 26 | M09 | | $1,463,013.24 |
| 27 | M10 | | $1,568,567.87 |
| 28 | M11 | | $1,596,141.88 |
| 29 | M12 | | $1,665,207.22 |
| 30 | **Grand Total** | **$28,207,295.63** | **$38,806,882.46** |

*Figure 4.21: Shifting dates.*

Now you can clearly see that for each cell, DAX uses the date range of the current cell to traverse time. This is one of the important reasons for including in your model a separate date table that contains a continuous date range.

For more information on this and similar concepts, see http://ppivot.us/KQSEF.

Jim chooses to create this calculation in the calculation area in Power Pivot. This way, he has easy access to all the other calculations in the model, and he has access to additional features such as hiding and showing calculated fields. Jim hides the calculated field he just created because he doesn't need this field to clutter the field list. He does so by right-clicking the field and selecting Hide from Client Tools.

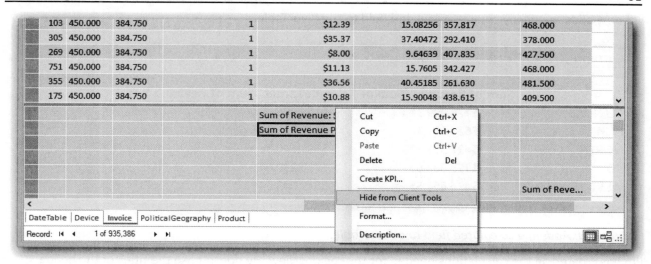

| | 103 | 450.000 | 384.750 | | 1 | $12.39 | 15.08256 | 357.817 | 468.000 | |
| | 305 | 450.000 | 384.750 | | 1 | $35.37 | 37.40472 | 292.410 | 378.000 | |
| | 269 | 450.000 | 384.750 | | 1 | $8.00 | 9.64639 | 407.835 | 427.500 | |
| | 751 | 450.000 | 384.750 | | 1 | $11.13 | 15.7605 | 342.427 | 468.000 | |
| | 355 | 450.000 | 384.750 | | 1 | $36.56 | 40.45185 | 261.630 | 481.500 | |
| | 175 | 450.000 | 384.750 | | 1 | $10.88 | 15.90048 | 438.615 | 409.500 | |

*Figure 4.22: Hiding a calculated field.*

Next, Jim creates the year-over-year calculation:

```
[Sum of Revenue YoY%] =
    IF(
        NOT(ISBLANK([Sum of Revenue])),
            DIVIDE(
                    ([Sum of Revenue]
                      - [Sum of Revenue PreviousYear])
                    ,[Sum of Revenue PreviousYear]
                )
        )
```

This calculation determines the year-over-year change when `[Sum of Revenue]` is not empty for the current cell; if it is empty, Power Pivot returns BLANK. When there is revenue for the current cell, Jim wants to use the DIVIDE function to divide the result of the subtraction of `[Sum of Revenue PreviousYear]` from `[Sum of Revenue]` by `[Sum of Revenue PreviousYear]`.

### Power Pivot Tip: The DIVIDE Function

The DIVIDE function was introduced in Power Pivot for SQL Server 2012 SP1 and Excel 2013. This function makes sure that either BLANK or an actual value is returned and is optimized for performance. When you use the / operator DAX has to handle the divide-by-zero error every time it happens resulting in a performance hit. The DIVIDE function is short-circuited to just return BLANK or an error value that you can optionally enter in the arguments when a divide-by-zero is encountered. It's recommended that you use the DIVIDE function whenever possible.

### Power Pivot Tip: BLANK Values?

A blank value, an empty cell, and a missing value are all represented by a special value type: BLANK. Why is this important? One of the main characteristics of working with data in Excel is that by default, blank values are never shown in PivotTables. So by returning a BLANK value by using the DAX BLANK() function, you can determine whether you want Excel to show something for the row or column for which your calculation is evaluated. This behavior has been mimicked by most client tools, such as Power View.

A blank value is treated a little differently in DAX than in Excel. For details, please see http://ppivot.us/JYCSL.

Jim now adds the newly created calculated field to the PivotTable.

| CurrentFyMonth 1 | | | |
|---|---|---|---|
| | **Sum of Revenue** | **Sum of RevenueTarget** | **Sum of Revenue YoY%** |
| CENTRAL | $176,989.31 | $154,005.25 | 42.64 % |
| EAST | $621,381.14 | $507,861.36 | 23.51 % |
| NORTH | $437,551.91 | $391,540.54 | 400.45 % |
| SOUTH | $178,088.65 | $136,230.04 | 1106.87 % |
| WEST | $426,652.55 | $349,042.04 | -52.28 % |

*Figure 4.23: Adding a calculated field to a PivotTable.*

Jim has created all the calculations needed for the regions view. He doesn't like the titles of the headers, so he changes them in the PivotTable. To do so, he selects a header and uses the formula bar to change the label. The calculated fields usually have very long names resulting in much unused white space in the PivotTabe, renaming the labels to a shorter label allows him to get rid of this whitespace and make it more understandable for the end users. He also centers the labels.

| CurrentFyMonth 1 | | | |
|---|---|---|---|
| | **Revenue** | **$VTT** | **YoY%** |
| CENTRAL | $176,989.31 | $154,005.25 | 42.64 % |
| EAST | $621,381.14 | $507,861.36 | 23.51 % |
| NORTH | $437,551.91 | $391,540.54 | 400.45 % |
| SOUTH | $178,088.65 | $136,230.04 | 1106.87 % |
| WEST | $426,652.55 | $349,042.04 | -52.28 % |

*Figure 4.24: Renamed PivotTable labels.*

Jim prefers the formatting done in Excel over the formatting set by the calculated fields in Power Pivot, so he sets the Revenue and $VTT columns to currency format and the YoY% column to percentage using the number settings on the home tab. For all columns, he removes the decimal numbers because on such large numbers, they don't add much value but take up a lot of space and make the numbers harder to read.

| CurrentFyMonth 1 | | | | |
|---|---|---|---|---|
| | **Revenue** | | **$VTT** | **YoY%** |
| CENTRAL | $ | 176,989 | $ 22,984 | 43% |
| EAST | $ | 621,381 | $ 113,520 | 24% |
| NORTH | $ | 437,552 | $ 46,011 | 400% |
| SOUTH | $ | 178,089 | $ 41,859 | 1107% |
| WEST | $ | 426,653 | $ 77,611 | -52% |

*Figure 4.25: Applied the appropriate formatting.*

## Dashboard Tip: Choosing the Right Precision

Here's another opportunity to make your information easier to digest: Determine what level of precision you need for the values you show. Dashboards usually present information at a very high level. Does it really make a difference if you show two decimal places? Or can you get rid of them? $45,223.12 and $45,223 tell the same story when you're talking about the revenue of an entire company. Of course, you should use your best judgment and not remove too much information. For example, in service-level agreements (SLAs), you probably want to see the difference between 99.34% and 99.96%, so you should keep the decimal places.

Changing the precision is easy to do, and you'll be surprised how much improvement this simple tip will gain you.

One of the things Jim has learned over the years is that it is important to make sure a PivotTable will not change layout whenever changes are made to the sheet, ruining the layout he has so painstakingly made. He therefore right-clicks the PivotTable and deselects Autofit Column Widths on Update.

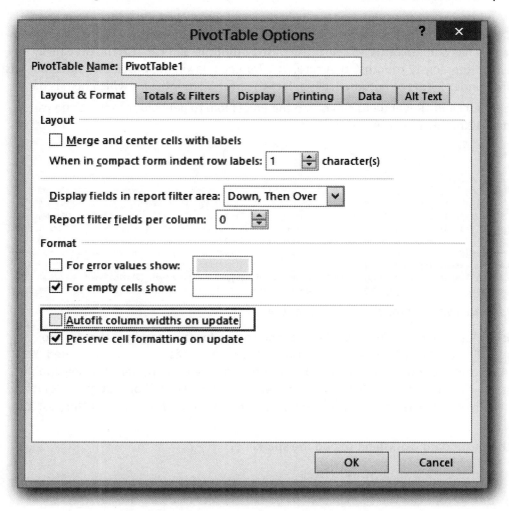

*Figure 4.26: Disabling autofit for columns in a PivotTable saves hassle later on.*

# Finding the Variance to Target Trend per Region for the Past 12 Months, Using Sparklines

In Jim's interviews with the board members, he learned that besides the information for each region for the current month, they also wanted to be able to see the trend. Jim wants to show for each region what the trend was for the past 12 months. He wants to do this in a small and inconspicuous way while still managing to convey the trend. He decides to create a sparkline that shows revenue for each region for the past 12 months. He wants to put the sparkline next to the PivotTable he created so that the two show data for the same regions.

To add a sparkline in Excel, Jim needs to use some special tricks. A sparkline needs to reference a range of cells, and you cannot create it by adding fields from the model, as you do in PivotTables. So Jim needs to indicate a range of cells that will create a range of values for each region for the past 12 months, based on the current month. He opens the DataSheet workbook he created earlier and creates a PivotTable there so he can reference it in the Dashboard sheet.

Jim adds regions to rows to represent the same regions as in the PivotTable. Next, he adds FyYear and Fy-Month under Columns because he wants to show the revenue for the past 12 months, counting back from the last month for which he has data. In order to select the past 12 months, Jim can use the previously created calculated column "Running 12 months" that returns 1 for each day in the past 12 months that has data. He adds this column under Filters to automatically select the past 12 months for which he has data.

Next, Jim adds the Calculated Field "Revenue to Target" to the PivotTable to get values for revenue variance to target for the past 12 months for which there is data.

| Running 12 months | 1 | ⊤ | | | | | | | | | |
|---|---|---|---|---|---|---|---|---|---|---|---|
| | | | | | | | | | | | |
| Revenue to target | Column Labels ▾ | | | | | | | | | | |
| | ⊟2012 | | | | | | | | 2012 Total | ⊟2013 | |
| Row Labels ▾ | 6 | 7 | 8 | 9 | 10 | 11 | 12 | | | 1 | |
| CENTRAL | ($9,935.30) | ($25,593.50) | ($28,353.05) | ($27,827.51) | ($17,273.32) | ($14,113.99) | ($7,252.35) | ($130,349.03) | ($2,971.66) | |
| EAST | ($7,293.61) | ($55,347.15) | ($78,347.42) | ($81,019.98) | ($36,755.05) | ($22,668.69) | $11,677.24 | ($269,754.66) | $27,088.91 | $30 |
| NORTH | ($32,819.89) | ($56,567.40) | ($74,104.90) | ($71,039.38) | ($45,821.08) | ($40,272.74) | ($17,201.29) | ($337,826.69) | ($9,814.07) | ($7, |
| SOUTH | ($11,520.36) | ($20,703.98) | ($24,940.45) | ($24,352.85) | ($13,703.18) | ($8,021.43) | ($23.87) | ($103,266.13) | $4,669.14 | $9 |
| WEST | ($4,641.29) | ($33,009.29) | ($48,371.46) | ($45,608.30) | ($21,482.37) | ($11,824.01) | $3,533.43 | ($161,403.29) | $22,606.09 | $22 |
| Grand Total | ($66,210.46) | ($191,221.32) | ($254,117.28) | ($249,848.02) | ($135,035.01) | ($96,900.86) | ($9,266.84) | ($1,002,599.80) | $41,578.42 | $55 |

*Figure 4.27: Revenue variance to target for the past 12 months.*

There is one small problem left: If Jim uses the PivotTable as the source for the sparkline, there is too much data. Since the sparkline uses a cell range, Jim needs to make sure he has 12 months returned. You might notice in Figure 4.27 that the total rows are also shown. Jim turns them off by selecting PivotTable Tools, Design, Subtotals, Do Not Show Subtotals and then he selects Design, Grand Totals, Off for Rows and Columns. This results in a PivotTable that just returns the regions and the sum of revenue for the past 12 months.

Jim now goes back to the DashBoard worksheet to add the sparkline.

## Dashboard Tip: Understanding Sparklines

Professor Edward Tufte introduced the sparkline in his book *Beautiful Evidence*. He says, "A sparkline is a small, intense, simple, word-sized graphic with typographic resolution. Sparklines mean that graphics are no longer cartoonish special occasions with captions and boxes, but rather sparkline graphics can be everywhere a word or number can be: embedded in a sentence, table, headline, map, spreadsheet, graphic."

Tufte invented the sparkline as a graphic that shows a trend in a space where you would usually have a label or text. A simple graphic shows trends much more clearly than does a range of numbers. Sparklines also save space on reports.

In Excel, three types of sparklines are available:

- **Line:** A line sparkline is usually used for chronological time series and other sequence values on the axis, such as stages of a production process. Line sparklines are very useful in helping spot changes or trends in data over time.

*Figure 4.28: A line sparkline.*

- **Column:** A column sparkline is usually used to compare amounts between specific discrete categorical values.

*Figure 4.29: A column sparkline.*

- **Win/loss:** A win/loss sparkline is special form of sparkline that shows whether data is positive (a win) or negative (a loss). This is great for showing stock tickers.

*Figure 4.30: A win/loss line sparkline.*

For more information, see this extensive Q&A on sparklines on Edward Tufte's website: http://ppivot.us/ZBPHS. For more examples of sparklines in Excel, see this great article full of examples from Bill Jelen: http://ppivot.us/GSEVU.

Jim decides to use a line sparkline because it shows the trend very clearly but is not too prominent. He moves the PivotTable one column to the right to create space for the sparkline and then clicks the Insert Sparkline button on the ribbon.

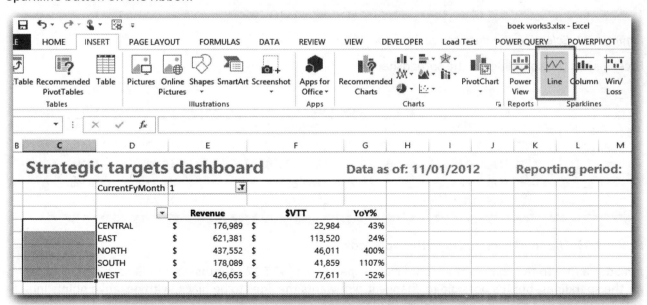

*Figure 4.31: Inserting a sparkline.*

The Create Sparklines dialog appears, and Jim needs to use it to select the data range for the values he wants to show. He selects the Data Range text box, switches to the DataSheet worksheet, and selects all the cells in the PivotTable.

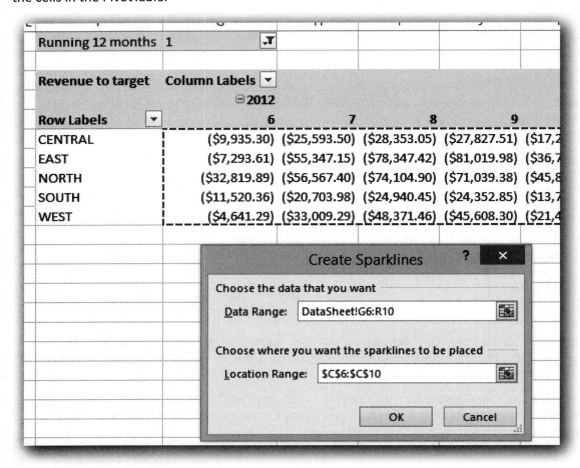

*Figure 4.32: Selecting the data range for a sparkline.*

Excel inserts the sparklines in the spreadsheet.

| | | Revenue | | $VTT | | YoY% |
|---|---|---|---|---|---|---|
| | CENTRAL | $ | 176,989 | $ | 22,984 | 43% |
| | EAST | $ | 621,381 | $ | 113,520 | 24% |
| | NORTH | $ | 437,552 | $ | 46,011 | 400% |
| | SOUTH | $ | 178,089 | $ | 41,859 | 1107% |
| | WEST | $ | 426,653 | $ | 77,611 | -52% |

*Figure 4.33: The sparklines added to the workbook.*

Jim adds a title to the column that contains the sparklines: $VTT 12 Months. Excel selects a default color for the sparklines, but it's possible to change it. Jim wants the lines to be black, with negative points indicated with red and the high point indicated with green.

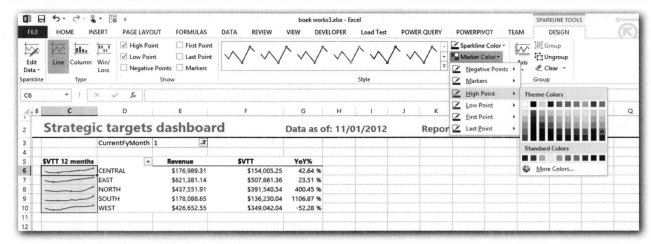

*Figure 4.34: Selecting custom sparkline colors.*

This great visual allows Jim to show the trend for each region over the past 12 months.

| $VTT 12 months | | Revenue | $VTT | YoY% |
|---|---|---|---|---|
| CurrentFyMonth | 1 | | | |
| | CENTRAL | $176,989.31 | $154,005.25 | 42.64 % |
| | EAST | $621,381.14 | $507,861.36 | 23.51 % |
| | NORTH | $437,551.91 | $391,540.54 | 400.45 % |
| | SOUTH | $178,088.65 | $136,230.04 | 1106.87 % |
| | WEST | $426,652.55 | $349,042.04 | -52.28 % |

*Figure 4.35: Sparklines applied to the report.*

From the dashboard that Jim has created, it's pretty clear that the targets have been met for all regions. Interestingly, the west region was the worst growth area. Maybe the target was not aggressive enough. It will surely provide enough material to generate some discussion in the next management meeting.

## Representing New Markets Reached in a PivotChart

The next report Jim wants to tackle is one to help gain insight into whether the marketing efforts in new markets have actually resulted in an increase in revenue in those new markets. Each region was responsible for its own marketing, and the board will want to see this split out by region.

Jim decides to show this by presenting the number of markets for which there have been sales over the past 12 months. He wants to use a graph, split out by region.

Jim adds a PivotChart to the report, directly besides the Region PivotTable he just created. He inserts a PivotChart and connects it to the workbook data model.

Next, he adds FyYearLabel and FyMonthLabel under Axis, Region under Legend, and Running 12 Months under Filters (to return only the past 12 months).

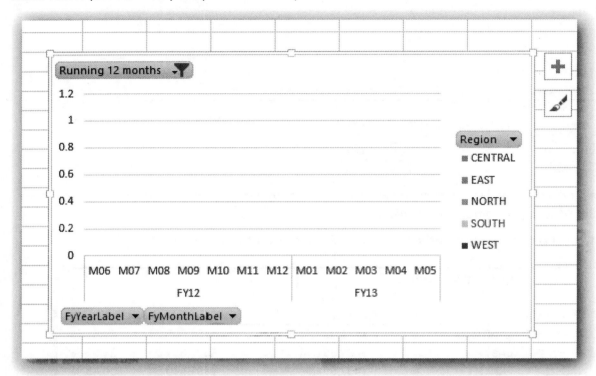

*Figure 4.36: Adding a PivotChart.*

To optimize his space, Jim decides to remove the field buttons. He removes the field buttons by selecting Analyze, Field Button, Hide All. Jim also decided to change the chart style to a line chart.

### Dashboard Tip: Choosing the Right Chart

Choosing the right chart to show data might be the hardest problem in data visualization. Unfortunately, there is no surefire way to choose the right chart. It depends on many, many factors— and on the data you want to show. You have to think about what information you want to show and what information is important. The core idea behind graphs and charts is that they help people understand data quickly and allow you to tell the story behind the data. Therefore, an important factor in choosing and designing the right chart is having a good understanding of the data and the types of charts.

There are four core types of chart visualizations: those that show the distribution of data points, those that make a comparison between data points, those that show the relationships between data points, and those that show how data points are put together (composition). These visualizations help your audience see what you are talking about.

Let's look at an example for each type:

• **Comparison:** You use this type when you want to compare two or more data points, such as the revenue for each month between years, revenue by region, or revenue for each month for the current year. This is the most common type and is usually a line, bar, or column chart.

• **Distribution:** This is the second most common chart category. As the name suggests, a distribution chart is used to display how data is distributed and to understand outliers and categories that are outside the norm (for example, distribution of voters per region, types of returned products over the past month).

• **Relationship:** This type shows interesting relationships that can lead to new understanding about correlations and causality between a wide ranges of variables. For example, you might use this type of chart if you want to prove whether hours of study make for better results or to show the relationship between in-store sales and holidays. The most common relationship charts are scatter plots and bubble charts.

- **Composition:** This type of chart allows you to display how specific data compares to broader data (for example, what browser types are visiting a website, product sales as a percentage of total revenue). Commonly used composition charts are column charts, bar charts, and pie charts.

When I'm trying to choose the right chart, I often use a graphic created by Andrew Abela: http://ppivot.us/TPXGX.

The next thing Jim does is add a calculated field for counting the number of distinct cities that have revenue. In the Invoice table, every Contoso Communications sales transaction creates a new row. Every row in the Transaction table contains a reference to where the transaction happened, and this information is stored in the PoliticalGeographyKey column. Here is Jim's calculated field for distinctly counting the markets:

```
[Nr of markets] =
DISTINCTCOUNT(Invoice[PoliticalGeographyKey])
```

The `DISTINCTCOUNT` function counts the distinct number of occurrences for each value of `PoliticalGeographyKey` in the Invoice table.

### Power Pivot Tip: Remembering That Context Is Always Applied

As mention in Chapter 3, it's important to remember the context where a calculation will be executed. The expression above will always calculate `DISTINCTCOUNT` for `Invoice[PoliticalGeographyKey]` for the values in that cell, filtered by what is on rows, columns, filters, and slicers. Whether you put regions, years, or products on rows, the value of `DISTINCTCOUNT` for `Invoice[PoliticalGeographyKey]` will automatically be calculated for the values that determine the context.

Adding this calculated field to the PivotChart gives Jim the chart shown in Figure 4.37.

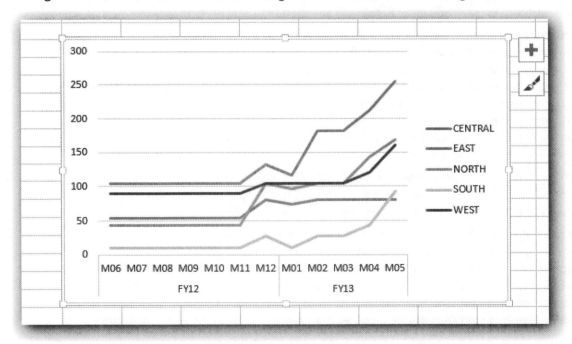

*Figure 4.37: Adding values to a PivotChart.*

Jim wants to align this chart perfectly with the PivotTable so he drags it while holding down the Alt key. The chart automatically snaps to the gridlines when it's placed on the grid. He also decides to align the legend to top to create more horizontal space, and he deselects Show the Legend Without Overlapping the Chart. He makes the chart a little wider on the x-axis and smaller on the y-axis. Finally, he changes the font to 10-point Segoe UI. He also sets the alignment of the chart to make sure the chart will align to the grid whenever he makes changes to other areas of the worksheet. To do this, he selects the chart and then selects the Page Layout Ribbon, Align, Snap to Grid. Jim now has a clear chart of the market growth over the past 12 months.

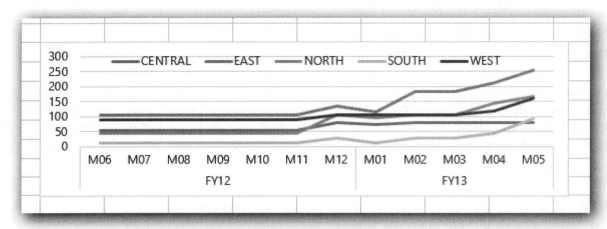

*Figure 4.38: The finished chart.*

## Dashboard Tip: Arranging Visuals

Good alignment of the major objects on a dashboard—like tables and charts—makes a big difference. The human brain gets distracted viewing objects that aren't aligned as it subconciously tries to align those objects instead of spending its cycles actually understanding the objects. In the 1920s, German psychologists including Kant and Goethe created what they called gestalt theories. *Gestalt* is German for "essence or shape of an entity's complete form." When applied to visual perception, these theories recognize that in order for the human brain to make sense of information, it tries to organize the information in a particular way. When humans look at a combination of visuals, we see the whole before we see the individual parts that make up that whole.

Early 20th-century psychologists determined that the fundamental principle of gestalt perception is the law of grouping. This law says that we tend to order our experience in a manner that is regular, orderly, symmetric, and simple. Those psychologists determined a number of principles that, in theory, would allow us to predict how a total visual is interpreted, including proximity, similarity, closure, symmetry, common fate, continuity, good gestalt, and experience. Following these principles helps you create a harmonious design that looks and feels right to the user. In recent years, these principles have become more and more important in the design world; many great designers use them intuitively.

You might be wondering "What does gestalt have to do with me? And how does it relate to the work I do in Excel?" Well, a complete study of this subject would fill a book on its own, but let's look at two important ideas that everyone should be able to apply:

• **Keep related data close:** If you have a PivotTable with revenue by region on your dashboard and you also have a chart that contains regions and revenue that either tells a different story or that supports the information on the PivotTable, make sure this information is grouped together. Such grouping reduces friction for the user: Seeing the same or similar information in close proximity makes it easier to understand. You may need to restructure a report or dashboard after you add additional pieces, and that can be a chore. But I assure you that it's well worth the effort.

• **Align everything:** Make sure all tables and charts are aligned and, if possible, of equal width and height. This will give your dashboard a much cleaner look and make it easier for the user to "grok" the information. Here a few simple tips for getting good alignment: First of all, when possible, start all your charts and tables on the same row and column when placed above or next to each other. If you set Snap to Grid for your charts, it will be easier to align them on the worksheet with other charts and tables. When everything is set to align to the worksheet's grid, it's a piece of cake to make objects the same width. Sometimes you need to get creative with charts to make them fit, but again, it's well worth it. Also, don't be afraid to leave some empty space between charts or tables; it's better to have some empty space than cram them together.

If you follow these two simple guidelines, your reports will be much easier to understand and read.

The following two examples show how you can quickly and easily get great results from some simple alignment.

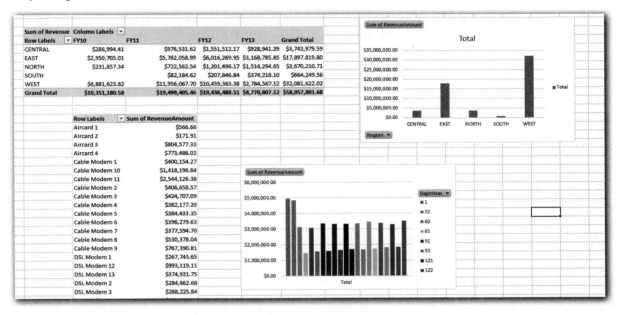

Figure 4.39: A busy report that's not aligned.

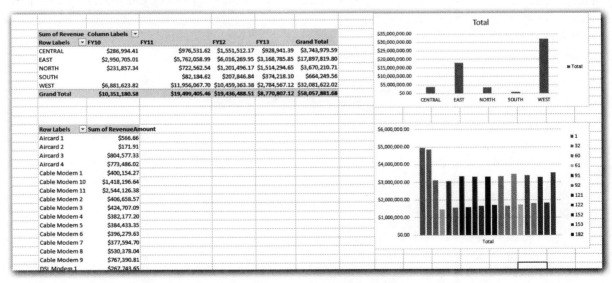

Figure 4.40: A report that contains the same data but is neat and organized.

For more information, see Stephen Few's books *Information Dashboard Design* and *Show Me the Numbers*.

# Reporting Dynamic Date Ranges Using Slicers

Jim wants to get some feedback on the first iteration of the dashboard from several business users who will be using the dashboard. The feedback is overwhelmingly positive, but one remark he hears multiple times is that the users wish they could see the reporting part of the dashboard reported over either the current month, quarter-to-date (QTD), or year-to-date (YTD). Jim decides that this is a great addition to his dashboard, and slicers will help him achieve it. Users will be able to select whatever they want to see.

To create slicers that a report user can select, Jim creates a new sheet called Variables in his workbook. Here he creates a table in Excel that contains Actual, QTD, and YTD rows.

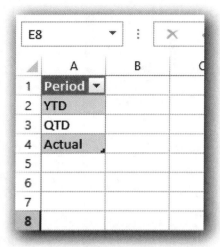

*Figure 4.41: A regular table in Excel.*

Jim now wants to add these values to the data model so he can reference the selection later, in a DAX formula. He selects the table and selects Insert, PivotTable. In the Create PivotTable dialog that appears, he selects Add This Data to the Data Model.

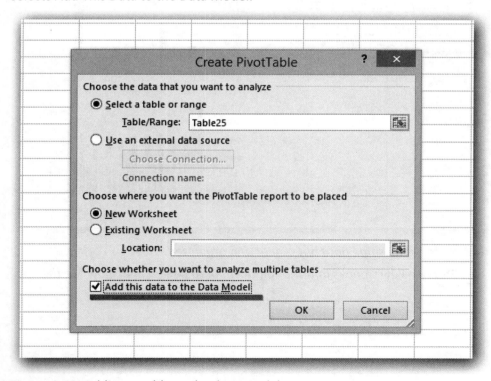

*Figure 4.42: Adding a table to the data model.*

Jim opens the Power Pivot add-in and renames the table varPeriod.

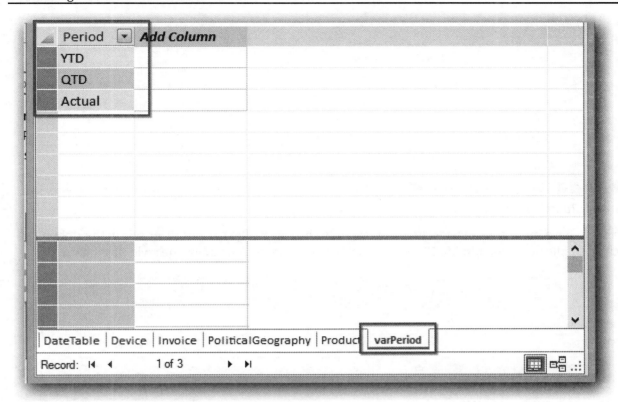

*Figure 4.43: The table visible in the data model.*

### Power Pivot Tip: Linked Tables

Linked tables in Power Pivot can be very powerful. They allow you to add any table from an Excel worksheet directly to the data model. This means you can add any data you typed into a table in Excel directly to the data model. When these tables are added to the data model, they become part of the refresh chain of the data model, which means whenever you refresh the data sources, the table loads new data from the text in the Excel table.

Imagine that you don't have sales targets for each product in your data source, but you have them available in a table in Excel. You can move the data into the data model and create relationships with the rest of your tables, and then you can combine data from the Sales table with the Targets table in any PivotTable. Then, whenever you make changes to any value in that table, you only have to refresh the table in PowerPivot or Excel, and the data is immediately refreshed in your model and PivotTables.

Jim can now use this data to create a slicer. He inserts a row between the reports and the headers and clicks Insert, Slicer. The Connections dialog appears, and in it Jim selects Data Model, Tables in Workbook Data Model. He then selects the Period column from the varPeriod table.

Jim changes the number of columns in the Slicer Tools Options tab from 1 to 3, and he drags the slicer to the area above the sparklines in the recently created row. Jim now decides to remove the label above the slicer, so he right-clicks the slicer and selects Slicer Options. In the Slicer Settings dialog that appears, Jim deselects Display Header. He also fine-tunes the width and height to his liking in the Slicer Tools Options tab.

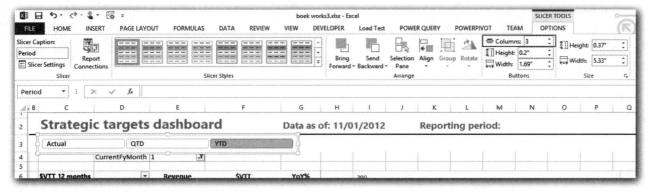

*Figure 4.44: Tuning a slicer.*

Jim wants to have more control over the slicer layout, so he selects the current slicer syle in the ribbon and right-clicks Duplicate. In the Modify Slicer Style dialog that appears, Jim names the style Dashboard.

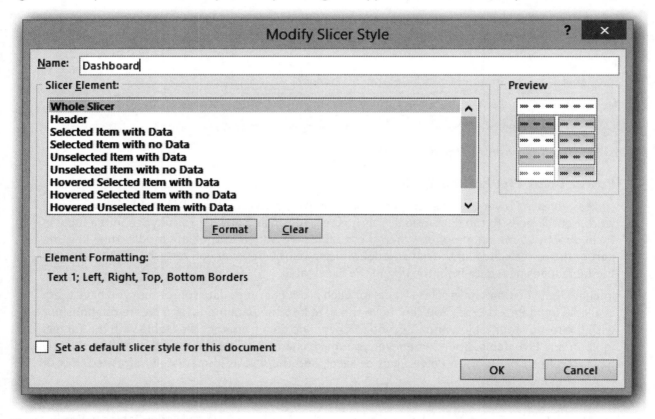

*Figure 4.45: Creating slicer styles.*

Jim selects the Whole Slicer option and clicks the Format button. Next, he sets the font to 10-point Segoe UI and the border to None. Then he selects Selected Item with Data and sets the fill color to match the header text. The slicer is now added to the worksheet.

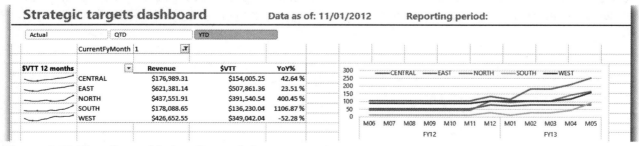

*Figure 4.46: The slicer added to the worksheet.*

Jim wants to use this slicer to determine the value in his PivotTable. Based on the slicer selection, he wants to show the actual, fiscal quarter-to-date, or fiscal year-to-date value for each calculation. Jim already has the values for actual, and he decides to add separate calculated fields for fiscal QTD and fiscal YTD.

He first adds a calculated field that determines the fiscal year-to-date sum of revenue:

```
[Sum of Revenue F YTD]=
IF(HASONEVALUE(DateTable[FyYear]),
    TOTALYTD([Sum of Revenue]
            ,DateTable[Date]
            ,"06/30")
    )
```

This calculation uses the [Sum of Revenue] calculated field for the entire YTD. The "to date" is based on the last date in the cell for which this calculated field is executed. The year is defined to end on June 30, making this work for a fiscal YTD. To make sure the calculation provides the right information per year, HASONEVALUE makes sure this calculation returns values only when there is only one DateTable[FyYear] selected.

Next, Jim creates a calculated field that uses Sum of Revenue F YTD to determine the fiscal year-to–date sum for the previous year:

```
[Sum of Revenue F YTD PreviousYear]=
IF(HASONEVALUE(DateTable[FyYear]),
    CALCULATE([Sum of Revenue F YTD]
            ,DATEADD(DateTable[Date]
                , -1
                , YEAR)
            )
    )
```

This calculation calculates [Sum of Revenue F YTD] for the entire YTD. But instead of using the date of the cell in the PivotTable, DATEADD moves this date back one year from the dates in the current cell selection.

Jim then creates a calculated field that determines the year-over-year growth by subtracting the revenue for the current fiscal YTD from the revenue for the previous fiscal YTD and divides the result by the revenue for the previous fiscal YTD when the current date selection has revenue:

```
[Sum of Revenue F YTD YoY%]=
IF(NOT(ISBLANK([Sum of Revenue])),
    DIVIDE([Sum of Revenue F YTD]
            - [Sum of Revenue F YTD PreviousYear]
        ,[Sum of Revenue F YTD PreviousYear])
    )
```

> The DIVIDE function is used to make sure that divide-by-zero errors will not be thrown. Instead, when these errors occur, a blank value will be returned.

Jim now uses the same technique to calculate the fiscal year-to-date sum of revenue target:

```
[Sum of Revenuetarget F YTD]=
 IF(HASONEVALUE(DateTable[FyYear]),
     TOTALYTD([Sum of Revenuetarget],
               DateTable[Date]
            ,"06/30")
        )
```

Finally he creates a calculated field to create fiscal year revenue to target by subtracting [Sum of Revenuetarget F YTD] from [Sum of Revenue F YTD]:

```
[Revenue to target F YTD]=
[Sum of Revenue F YTD]-[Sum of Revenuetarget F YTD]
```

Jim creates the same calculation for fiscal quarter-to-date:

```
[Sum of Revenue F QTD] =
 IF(HASONEVALUE(DateTable[FYQuarter]),
     TOTALQTD([Sum of Revenue]
               ,DateTable[Date])
        )
```

> Because fiscal quarters usually don't run differently from normal quarters, you can use the TOTALQTD function.

To calculate Revenue to target F QTD and Sum of Revenue F QTD YoY%, Jim uses the same calculation pattern as for the YTD measures but swaps out the Sum of Revenue F YTD calculated field for Sum of Revenue F QTD.

Now that Jim added calculated fields to calculate revenue, variance to target, and year-over-year growth for the current month, fiscal QTD, and fiscal YTD, he needs to find a way to make the values on his report respect the slicer he just created. Jim therefore creates a calculated field that he can use in all other calculated fields to check whether the slicer has only one value selected. He doesn't want to show any value when the user selects both YTD and QTD. He creates a calculated field that will check whether the slicer has only one value selected:

```
[isReportSlicerSet]=
 HASONEVALUE(varPeriod[Period])
```

> This calculated field uses the HASONEVALUE function to return true or false, depending on whether varPeriod[Period] has one value for the current cell where the calculation field is executed in the PivotTable.

Before he continues, Jim hides the calculated field because he doesn't need it in anything except as a building block in other calculated fields.

Jim now creates a calculated field that returns a result based on the value of the slicer:

```
RevenueByPeriod =
  IF([isReportSlicerSet],
     SWITCH(VALUES(varPeriod[Period]),
         "Actual",[Sum of Revenue],
         "YTD",[Sum of Revenue F YTD],
         "QTD",[Sum of Revenue F QTD]
         )
      )
```

> When the `isReportSlicerSet` calculated field returns `true`, you use the `VALUES` function to determine the current value for `varPeriod[Period]` for this PivotTable. If you didn't check for the single value of `varPeriod[Period]` and the user selected multiple values in the slicer, the `VALUES` function would return an error because it wouldn't return a single value. You then use the `SWITCH` statement to determine which calculated field will be executed, based on the value of `varPeriod[Period]`.

### Power Pivot Tip: The VALUES Function

The `VALUES` function allows you to use values in the current context of the PivotTable. Consider the follow DAX formula:

```
[Test Value]=
            =IF(HASONEVALUE(PoliticalGeography[Region]) &&
               HASONEVALUE(DateTable[FyYearLabel]),
               VALUES(PoliticalGeography[Region]) &
               " " &
               VALUES(DateTable[FyYearLabel]))
```

This formula shows the value of `PoliticalGeography[Region]` and `DateTable[FyYearLabel]` in each cell in the PivotTable where the cell only has one value for each.

| | | | | | |
|---|---|---|---|---|---|
| 2 | | | | | |
| 3 | **Calculated field 1** | **Column Labels** ▼ | | | |
| 4 | **Row Labels** ▼ | **FY10** | **FY11** | **FY12** | **FY13** | **FY14** |
| 5 | CENTRAL | CENTRAL FY10 | CENTRAL FY11 | CENTRAL FY12 | CENTRAL FY13 | CENTRAL FY14 |
| 6 | EAST | EAST FY10 | EAST FY11 | EAST FY12 | EAST FY13 | EAST FY14 |
| 7 | NORTH | NORTH FY10 | NORTH FY11 | NORTH FY12 | NORTH FY13 | NORTH FY14 |
| 8 | SOUTH | SOUTH FY10 | SOUTH FY11 | SOUTH FY12 | SOUTH FY13 | SOUTH FY14 |
| 9 | WEST | WEST FY10 | WEST FY11 | WEST FY12 | WEST FY13 | WEST FY14 |
| 10 | | | | | | |
| 11 | | | | | | |

*Figure 4.47: the* VALUES *function is used to show the context*

You can use the `VALUES` function in many situations, such as in a running sum, where you use it to get the current month to determine the time range for a calculation.

Jim repeats the same pattern for variation from target and year-over–year revenue. Then he replaces the calculated fields from the PivotTable with the newly created calculated fields.

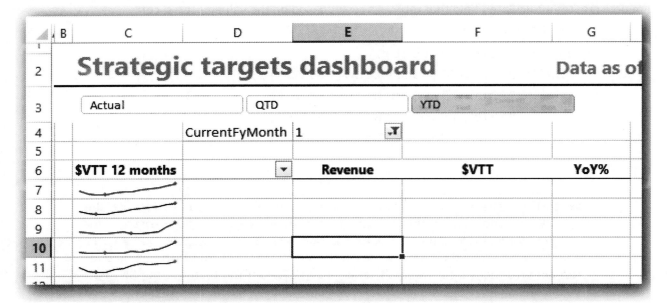

*Figure 4.48: The new calculated fields added to the report.*

There is one thing missing here: The calculated fields don't return any value, even though Jim has selected a single value in the slicer. In order for the calculated fields in the PivotTable to pick up the slicer, Jim needs to connect the slicer to the PivotTable. Jim selects the PivotTable, goes to PivotTable Tools, and selects Slicer Connections. The Filter Connections dialog that appears allows Jim to manually tell Excel which slicers are connected to this PivotTable.

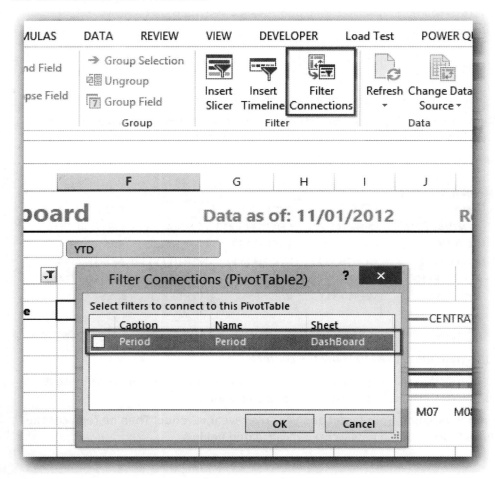

*Figure 4.49: Creating a slicer connection to a PivotTable.*

He checks the Period slicer and clicks OK. Now the calculated fields show the values he expects.

| Actual | | QTD | | YTD | | |
|---|---|---|---|---|---|---|
| | CurrentFyMonth 1 | | | | | |
| $VTT 12 months | ▼ | Revenue | | $VTT | | YoY% |
| ∿ | CENTRAL | $ | 928,941 | $ | 47,083 | 46% |
| ∿ | EAST | $ | 3,168,786 | $ | 337,650 | 23% |
| ∿ | NORTH | $ | 1,514,295 | $ | 25,077 | 237% |
| ∿ | SOUTH | $ | 374,218 | $ | 89,044 | 398% |
| ∿ | WEST | $ | 2,784,567 | $ | 192,890 | -40% |

*Figure 4.50: Values in the PivotTable now show up*

The last thing Jim wants to do is hook up the Reporting Period title to the slicer to report the right report-ing period, based on the slicer. He is going to use traditional Excel functions to get the results, so he needs to make sure he has access to values. He adds the period to the PivotTable on the DataSheet worksheet. Because he will need the quarter label as well, he also adds that to the PivotTable. He also connects the slicer to this PivotTable.

| | A | B | C | D |
|---|---|---|---|---|
| 1 | CurrentFyMonth  1 | | | |
| 2 | | | | |
| 3 | Row Labels | Absolute Last Invoice Date | Current date | |
| 4 | ⊟FY13 | 11/1/2012 | 9/21/2013 19:46 | |
| 5 | ⊟M05 | 11/1/2012 | 9/21/2013 19:46 | |
| 6 | ⊟Q2 | 11/1/2012 | 9/21/2013 19:46 | |
| 7 | YTD | 11/1/2012 | 9/21/2013 19:46 | |
| 8 | Grand Total | 11/1/2012 | 9/21/2013 19:46 | |
| 9 | | | | |

*Figure 4.51: The DataSheet worksheet, with the value of the slicer added.*

Jim now adds the following Excel formula to the title:

```
="Reporting period:  "&
  IF(DataSheet!A7="Actual",
    DataSheet!A4 &" " &DataSheet!A5,
      IF(DataSheet!A7="QTD",
        DataSheet!A4 &" " &DataSheet!A6
 ,DataSheet!A4))
```

This Excel function gets values from different places on a PivotTable, based on the value of cell DataSheet!A7. This cell on the PivotTable represent the value of the slicer. Based on this value, the function will get values from the cell where Jim added year, month, and quarter labels

This function creates a label that reacts to slicer clicks.

| Strategic targets dashboard | | Data as of: 11/01/2012 | | Reporting period: FY13 |

| Actual | QTD | YTD | | |

| | CurrentFyMonth | 1 | | |

| $VTT 12 months | | Revenue | $VTT | YoY% | | 300 | CENTRAL — EAST — NORTH — SOUTH |
| | CENTRAL | $     928,941 | $        47,083 | 46% | | 250 | |

*Figure 4.52: The title reacts to slicer clicks.*

## Creating an Actuals Versus Budget Report

The next part of the dashboard is really the centerpiece of the report. One of the most important require-ments is to be able to see the rhythm of the business for each key metric for the current month, current QTD, and current fiscal YTD. The key metrics of the business are revenue, units, usage, and subscribers. For each of these metrics, Jim needs to show the actuals, variance to target, and year-over-year growth for each time period in the report. This report needs to be connected to the slicer he just created.

Jim has been creating these reports for years and knows what to do. He knows that regular PivotTables are unable to achieve the type of layout he needs, so he has to use a different approach. The report has to show up at the top of the report, so Jim creates the report framework by adding the fields he needs to the worksheet above the piece of the report he just created. He makes sure the reports are aligned properly and have the same style.

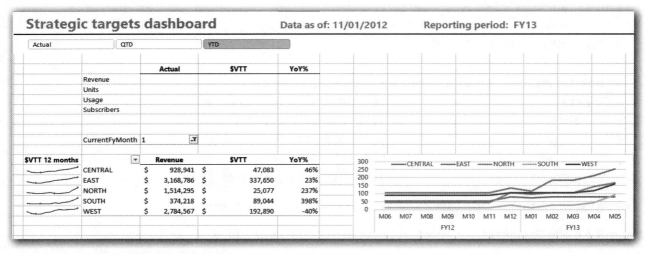

*Figure 4.53: Creating the framework for the report.*

Jim now wants to add the values of the metrics to the report. He decides to use another PivotTable on the DataSheet worksheet that he can then use as source for his report in the layout he chose.

In the DataSheet worksheet, Jim adds a new PivotTable. The basis of the report is the current month, so he adds CurrentFyMonth under Filter and selects 1 there. This PivotTable needs to use the dynamic date range again, so he connects the slicers and adds the calculations for Revenue, Revenue VTT, and Revenue YoY%. Jim also decides to put the values on rows to ensure that the calculations appear vertically in the PivotTable, which will make maintaining the DataSheet worksheet a little easier. Now any calculation he adds is added on rows instead of columns. This makes maintaining a large list of calculations easier to do.

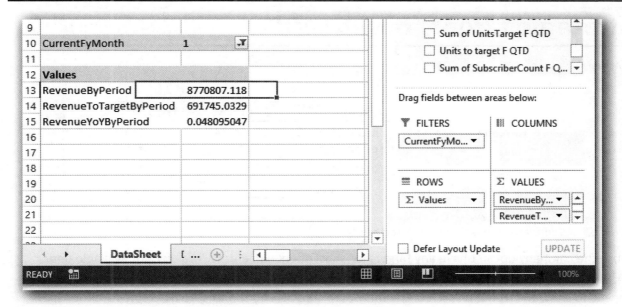

*Figure 4.54: Creating the PivotTable as a data source for a report.*

Jim now adds these calculated fields to the DashBoard worksheet by selecting the cell where he wants to add the value and typing the = sign in the formula bar. Next, he selects the DataSheet worksheet and clicks the RevenueByPeriod value in the PivotTable shown in the figure above. Jim gets the following formula:

```
=GETPIVOTDATA("[Measures].[RevenueByPeriod]"
                ,DataSheet!$A$12)
```

### Excel Tip: The `GETPIVOTDATA` Function

The Excel `GETPIVOTDATA` function returns data stored in a PivotTable report. It can return any value from the PivotTable, as long as it is visible. Learn more about this function from MrExcel: http://ppivot.us/WJEVB.

Jim continues adding calculated fields to the data model for units, usage, and subscribers, using the same calculation template he created for revenue.

### Power Pivot Tip: Making a Template of Your Calculated Fields

You will likely find that you create the same calculated fields over and over, with just small variations, just as Jim did. In his case, Jim used a different base calculated field, but the rest stayed the same. Keep this in the back of your mind when you design your calculated fields. It is important to split up your calculated fields into smaller calculations and reuse those building blocks wherever possible. Also, make sure to hide the intermediate calculations when you don't think there is going to be a need for them in your PivotTables. Hidden calculations will not show in the field list, but you will be able to reference them in other calculations.

Jim adds the references to the worksheet and applies the appropriate formatting.

## Strategic targets dashboard      Data as of: 11/(

| Actual | QTD | YTD |
|--------|-----|-----|

|  | Actual | $VTT | YoY% |
|--------|--------|------|------|
| Revenue | $       8,770,807 | $         691,745 | 5% |
| Units | 1,194,362,760 | (24,817,276) | -5% |
| Usage | 993,872,639 | 91,635,628 | 0% |
| Subscribers | 419,558 |  | -7% |

*Figure 4.55: Adding the remaining calculated fields.*

Because the company doesn't have any targets for subscribers, Jim enters "n/a" for not available under $VTT for Subscribers.

Jim wants to show the trend for each of the metrics for the past 12 months, so he creates another sparkline. To do this, he creates a PivotTable in the DataSheet worksheet, where he adds Running 12 Months under Filter and adds Sum of Revenue, Sum of Units, Sum of Usage, and Sum of SubscriberCount under Values. Finally, he adds Year and Month under Columns and moves the Σ Values item from the Columns to Rows.

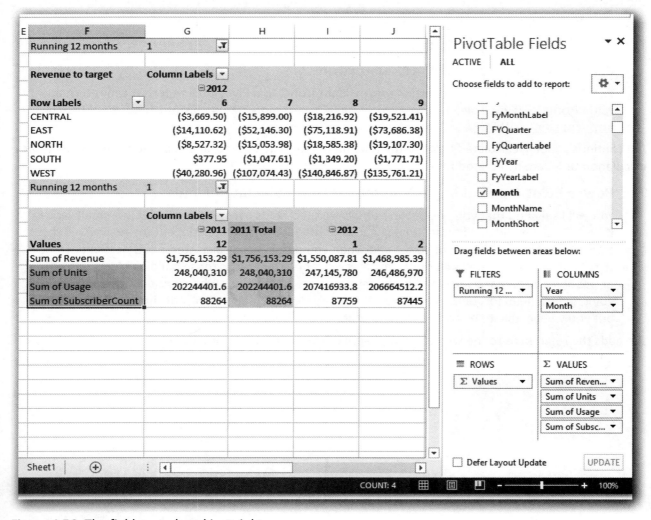

*Figure 4.56: The fields are placed just right.*

He then removes the subtotals and grand totals from the PivotTable and creates the sparklines, based on the values in the PivotTable, exactly as he did for the sparkline for variance to target.

## Strategic targets dashboard          Data as of: 11/01/2012

| Actual | | QTD | | YTD | |
|---|---|---|---|---|---|

| | | Actual | $VTT | YoY% |
|---|---|---|---|---|
| | Revenue | $ 8,770,807 | $ 691,745 | 5% |
| | Units | 1,194,362,760 | (24,817,276) | -5% |
| | Usage | 993,872,639 | 91,635,628 | 0% |
| | Subscribers | 419,558 | n/a | -7% |

*Figure 4.57: Creating a second set of sparklines in the dashboard.*

Both the sparkline and the YoY% field show clearly how the business has been doing over the past 12 months.

## Making a $VTT PivotChart for the Past 12 Months

Jim wants to make the revenue over the past 12 months even more pronounced in the report. To accomplish this, he's going to add a new chart that shows $VTT over the past 12 months. He adds a PivotChart above to the report he just created and aligns the two well.

### Dashboard Tip: Choosing the Right Calculation

Another tip that will allow you to make your reports more readable is to take a good look at the calculations you use in your charts. Remember that if you can convey the same information with fewer visuals, your report will be easier to read. For example, say that you want to compare values with targets If you want to visualize this, you will probably create a bar chart with revenue and revenue target by fiscal year.

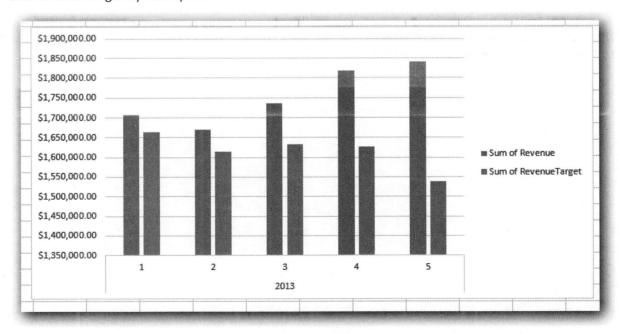

*Figure 4.58: Showing both revenue and revenue target by fiscal year.*

This chart allows you to see that the revenue has been outpacing the revenue target for the past couple years. However, you need to take some time to read the labels and look at the information up close. Now, if you show the same information in a different way—subtracting revenue target from revenue in a calculated field and creating a line chart out of that—it is much easier to see that the revenue has been growing more quickly than the revenue target over the past couple years, just by looking at the shape of the line.

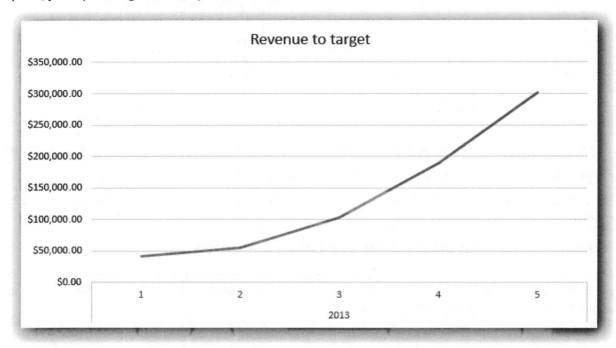

*Figure 4.59: The same information shown as a single line.*

Of course, you have to use good judgment here and make sure you don't get rid of too much information. How much you use depends on what you want to visualize. If you want to create a chart that shows revenue and revenue target, you might want to keep the bar charts. But if the goal is to show revenue compared to revenue target, the single line is much clearer—although it doesn't allow you to see how much revenue was made.

Jim adds FyYearLabel and FyMonthLabel under Axis and Running 12 Months under Filters. He sets the filter to 1 and adds the revenue to the target calculated field.

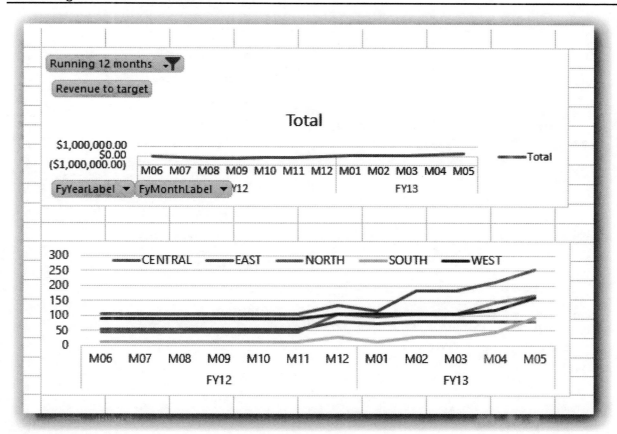

*Figure 4.60: Created the initial chart, it needs some work.*

Jim now starts cleaning up the chart. He removes the buttons by selecting PivotChart Tools, Analyze, Field Buttons, Hide All. He then removes the legend and the title of the chart. Next, he sets the chart axis format because he doesn't need the entire value to show. Jim right-clicks Axis and selects Format Axis. Next, he chooses to display the units in thousands, deselects Show Display Units Label on Chart, and then changes the formatting of the value to $#,##0 K. This provide his own custom number formatting, it will show numbers in the thousands followed by the letter K to represent thousand.

He then aligns the plot area of the chart with the chart below to make sure the months and years are in sync. This improves readability and makes the charts and tables look tidy.

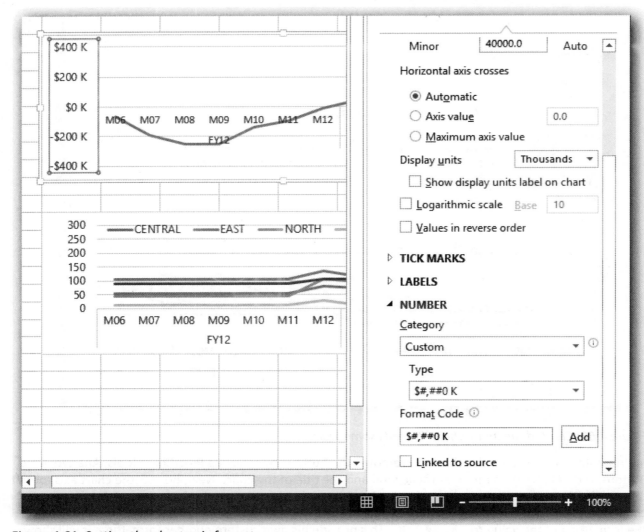

*Figure 4.61: Setting the chart axis format.*

The last thing Jim does on this chart is change the color scheme by selecting the chart and then selecting PivotChart Tools, Design, Change Colors and pick Color 3 to make the line readable.

Jim also wants the user to clearly see the trend, so he selects the line in the chart, right-clicks, and selects Add Trendline.

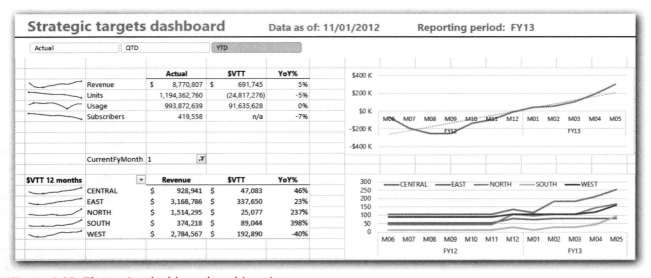

*Figure 4.62: The entire dashboard at this point.*

## Dashboard Tip: Labeling Appropriately

In order for the user to differentiate the different reports onscreen, it is important to provide appropriate information and label the areas clearly and concisely. As mentioned earlier, is important that a label not compete with the information being displayed. Using a lighter hue for the text color solves this problem.

Jim now adds labels to his reports and PivotCharts.  He uses a slightly larger font for the labels and makes the color the same as the report title.

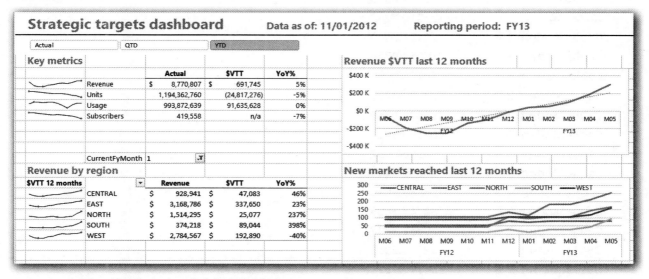

*Figure 4.63: The dashboard with labels added.*

# Identifying Top Devices by Revenue

One of the marketing teams has been working on promoting the top-selling products. Jim wants to create a table that shows the sales for the 10 best-selling products by revenue, their percentage of the total, and their percentage year-over-year growth.

Jim adds a new PivotTable to the dashboard, directly below the Region PivotTable. To this new PivotTable he adds DeviceName and Sum of Revenue. Jim uses the `Sum of Revenue by Period` calculated field he created earlier because he wants this PivotTable to also react to the slicer. He connects the slicer to the PivotTable, and he sees that the PivotTable is empty. He remembers that because he used the time intelligence functions, he needs to select a base period for the functions to work. He adds a filter that selects current month. Now he sees data getting returned. He also changes the PivotTable style to the one called None.

| CurrentFyMonth | 1 | ▼ |
| --- | --- | --- |

| Row Labels | ▼ | RevenueByPeriod |
| --- | --- | --- |
| Aircard 1 | | 167.5439 |
| Aircard 2 | | 47.3784 |
| Aircard 3 | | 121141.8315 |
| Aircard 4 | | 121219.7248 |
| Cable Modem 1 | | 71451.9469 |
| Cable Modem 10 | | 216552.9756 |
| Cable Modem 11 | | 361073.695 |
| Cable Modem 2 | | 72294.3216 |
| Cable Modem 3 | | 75429.6789 |
| Cable Modem 4 | | 65166.9411 |
| Cable Modem 5 | | 68964.997 |
| Cable Modem 6 | | 68656.3444 |
| Cable Modem 7 | | 64891.015 |
| Cable Modem 8 | | 88747.5693 |
| Cable Modem 9 | | 120662.9817 |
| DSL Modem 1 | | 32910.3365 |
| DSL Modem 12 | | 154799.4578 |
| DSL Modem 13 | | 62767.3722 |
| DSL Modem 2 | | 38180.1673 |
| DSL Modem 3 | | 38410.4274 |
| DSL Modem 4 | | 38575.6137 |
| DSL Modem 5 | | 33458.6171 |
| DSL Modem 6 | | 32834.3623 |
| DSL Modem 7 | | 32949.254 |

*Figure 4.64: A PivotTable for devices and revenue.*

To get the top 10 devices by revenue, Jim uses the native PivotTable filtering and ordering. He clicks the arrow at the row header to open the drop-down, where he can set a filter on the values to sort by top 10.

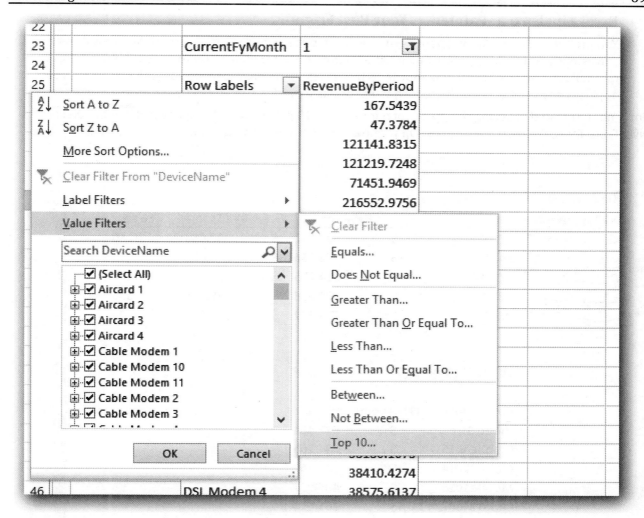

Figure 4.65: Using PivotTable sorting and filtering.

He wants to show only the top 10 items for ProductName by Revenue.

Figure 4.66: Selecting the top 10 filter for the PivotTable

Jim now sees just 10 products in the PivotTable instead of the entire list. There are two issues with the result. The first is that the products are not sorted. Jim clicks the arrow at the row header again and then selects Sort by Z to A to see the product with the most revenue at the top. The other problem is that the formatting is not the formatting used in the rest of the dashboard. In order to apply the same formatting everywhere, Jim selects the Revenue column in the Region PivotTable, clicks the Format Painter button, and selects all rows in the Revenue by Products PivotTable. The formatting applied to the Revenue column in the Region PivotTable is copied to the second PivotTable.

### Excel Tip: Format Painter . . . Your Best Friend!

You probably already know about Format Painter, but I want to emphasize the fact that using it consistently will make your life much easier. Format Painter allows you to copy the format from one cell (or a range of cells) into another. This makes it very easy to make sure the formatting you apply is consistent all over the report, table, or dashboard.

Jim is not interested in seeing the grand total for the top 10 products, so he removes those by selecting PivotTable Tools, Design, Grand Totals, Off for Rows and Columns. This gives him the PivotTable he wants.

| CurrentFyMonth | 1 | | | | |
|---|---|---|---|---|---|
| **Revenue by region** | | | | | |
| **$VTT 12 months** | ▼ | **Revenue** | | **$VTT** | **YoY%** |
| | CENTRAL | $ | 928,941 | $ | 47,083 | 46% |
| | EAST | $ | 3,168,786 | $ | 337,650 | 23% |
| | NORTH | $ | 1,514,295 | $ | 25,077 | 237% |
| | SOUTH | $ | 374,218 | $ | 89,044 | 398% |
| | WEST | $ | 2,784,567 | $ | 192,890 | -40% |

| CurrentFyMonth | 1 | |
|---|---|---|
| Row Labels | RevenueByPeriod | |
| Video Stream | $ | 677,484 |
| Mobile1015 | $ | 544,265 |
| Mobile1014 | $ | 534,757 |
| Mobile1018 | $ | 407,957 |
| Cable Modem 11 | $ | 361,074 |
| Mobile1017 | $ | 338,460 |
| Mobile1016 | $ | 335,702 |
| Premium Phone | $ | 269,727 |
| Cable Modem 10 | $ | 216,553 |
| MT 1010 | $ | 209,208 |

*Figure 4.67: The top 10 devices by revenue.*

Next, Jim adds year-over-year growth by simply adding the RevenueYoYByPeriod calculated field to the PivotTable and applying the same the formatting as for YoY% in the Region table.

| CurrentFyMonth | 1 | .T | |
|---|---|---|---|

| Row Labels | .T | RevenueByPeriod | RevenueYoYByPeriod |
|---|---|---|---|
| Video Stream | $ | 677,484 | 5% |
| Mobile1015 | $ | 544,265 | 119% |
| Mobile1014 | $ | 534,757 | 110% |
| Mobile1018 | $ | 407,957 | -1% |
| Cable Modem 11 | $ | 361,074 | -5% |
| Mobile1017 | $ | 338,460 | 4% |
| Mobile1016 | $ | 335,702 | -2% |
| Premium Phone | $ | 269,727 | -3% |
| Cable Modem 10 | $ | 216,553 | 1% |
| MT 1010 | $ | 209,208 | -10% |

*Figure 4.68: The top 10 devices by revenue and YoY%.*

Now, for the percentage of total, Jim wants to add a new calculated field to calculate the revenue for one device compared to the revenue for all devices. Jim adds a calculated field that calculates the revenue for all devices:

```
[Revenue all products]=
CALCULATE([Sum of Revenue],ALL(Product))
```

> This calculated field determines the sum of revenue for all products, regardless of any filters on Product.

Jim decides that he probably will never use the [Revenue all products] calculated field directly in his PivotTable, so he hides it. Now that he has this value, he can divide the sum of revenue for the current product by the revenue for all products:

```
[Pct of all products]=
DIVIDE([Sum of Revenue], [Revenue all products])
```

> This calculated field divides the sum of revenue for the current product by the revenue for all products.

Jim adds the calculated field to the PivotTable and applies appropriate formatting. He uses the font style he created to apply a consistent font to the PivotTable. He also adds the correct column headers and adds the line between column headers and the rows. Finally, he adds the label Top 10 Devices by Revenue to the PivotTable, which gives Jim the results he expects.

| | | | | | |
|---|---|---|---|---|---|
| ⟋ | EAST | $ | 3,168,786 | $ | 337,650 | 23% |
| ⟋ | NORTH | $ | 1,514,295 | $ | 25,077 | 237% |
| ⟋ | SOUTH | $ | 374,218 | $ | 89,044 | 398% |
| ⟋ | WEST | $ | 2,784,567 | $ | 192,890 | -40% |

| | |
|---|---|
| CurrentFyMonth | 1 |

## Top 10 devices by revenue

| | Revenue | % to total | YoY% |
|---|---|---|---|
| Video Stream | $ 677,484 | 8% | 5% |
| Mobile1015 | $ 544,265 | 8% | 119% |
| Mobile1014 | $ 534,757 | 8% | 110% |
| Mobile1018 | $ 407,957 | 5% | -1% |
| Cable Modem 11 | $ 361,074 | 4% | -5% |
| Mobile1017 | $ 338,460 | 4% | 4% |
| Mobile1016 | $ 335,702 | 4% | -2% |
| Premium Phone | $ 269,727 | 3% | -3% |
| Cable Modem 10 | $ 216,553 | 2% | 1% |
| MT 1010 | $ 209,208 | 2% | -10% |

*Figure 4.69: The top 10 devices report.*

Clearly, some products have failed to grow substantially, while others have grown astronomically. The board will want to investigate the reasons behind this.

## Showing Revenue per Unit Year-over-Year Growth in a PivotChart

One of the important requests from the board was to be able to see if the cost reduction has had an effect this fiscal year. Jim decides to show this by displaying the revenue per unit compared to the same revenue per unit in the previous year. He will show the numbers in a simple line chart.

Jim already created a `[Sum of Units]` calculated field, and now he creates a calculated field that will divide the revenue by the number of units:

```
[Revenue by Units]=
 DIVIDE([Sum of Revenue],[Sum of Units])
```

Next, he wants to get the revenue by units from the previous year:

```
[Revenue by Units Previous Year]=
 IF(HASONEVALUE(DateTable[FyYear]),
  CALCULATE([Revenue by Units],
         SAMEPERIODLASTYEAR(DateTable[Date])
         )
   )
```

This calculation uses the CALCULATE function to change the date range for the current cell context to the previous year by passing the SAMEPERIODLASTYEAR function as a parameter for CALCULATE. Jim wants to make sure that this calculated field can be used only when a single year is selected, so he uses the HASONEVALUE function to check whether the current cell really contains only a single year. As you note we now use SAMEPERIODLASTYEAR instead of DATEADD, these are actually the same. SAMEPERIODLASTYEAR is just a shorthand notation for ease of use.

Now that Jim has both the revenue by units for the current period and the revenue by units for the previous year, he can calculate the year-over-year growth:

```
[Revenue by Units YoY%]=
IF([Revenue by Units]>0,
        DIVIDE([Revenue by Units]
            -[Revenue by Units Previous Year]
        ,[Revenue by Units Previous Year])
    )
```

Because Jim wants to make sure the percentage will be calculated only when there is revenue by units for the current period, he uses the `IF` function in the calculation.

Jim inserts a PivotChart in the dashboard, aligned to the bottom right. Because the board wants to see the growth for the current fiscal year, he adds the DateTable[Running 12 months] field under Filter and selects 1. Next, he adds DateTable[FyYearLabel] and DateTable[FyMonthLabel] under Axis and adds the newly created calculated field [Revenue by Units YoY%] under Values.

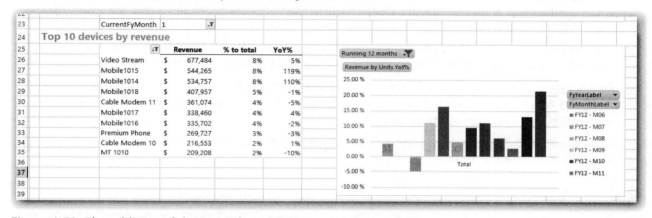

*Figure 4.70: The addition of the PivotChart for year-over-year revenue.*

This chart shows values over a period of time, so Jim changes the chart type to a line chart. He also chooses to make the chart less intrusive by using a subtle orange color that he selects in the Design tab. Jim removes the chart title and the format legend, and he hides the chart buttons. Finally, he adds a label to the chart: Revenue by Unit YoY% Past 12 Months. This gives him a chart that clearly shows that the cost cuts made a difference: The revenue by units is up by 25%.

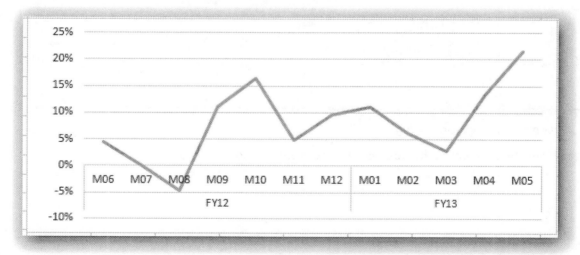

*Figure 4.71: The PivotChart clearly shows the YoY percentage change over time.*

# Bringing Focus to Parts of the Report That Need Attention

Jim wants to make sure that the board members are able to detect any numbers that they have to take action on.

## Dashboard Tip: Bringing Attention Where Attention Is Warranted (KPI's)

The KPI is famous and is almost synonymous with *dashboard*. KPI stands for *key performance indicator* and is developed to gauge the success or failure of a metric it is associated with. Originally, companies used KPIs to keep track of the key metrics of the business for a period, even before reports and computers became mainstream. In business intelligence, a KPI is usually associated with a visualization such as a traffic light that shows red, green, or yellow to indicate the status of the metric. This visualization is usually a default control or feature in most data visualization tools, including Excel, Power Pivot, and SQL Server Reporting Services.

I usually prefer to abstain from using KPIs, in the traditional BI sense of the word, in my dashboards. Instead, I rely on other visualization methods to bring attention to parts of a dashboard that need the user's immediate attention. When you have an entire dashboard littered with red, green, and yellow colors, it becomes very hard to see anything and can't bring attention to a metric that is off target and needs immediate attention. When a metric is on target, does it need to draw attention with a big green icon or green background? Usually the answer is no, but sometimes the answer is yes, depending on the importance of the measure or business requirements.

Remember that the customer is always boss. Some CFOs or dashboard users expect and want their KPIs to be green when the metrics are on or over target. You should give them what they want if they are not open to other ideas.

Jim selects the YoY% cells from the key metric part of the report and selects Home, Conditional Formatting, Highlight Cells Rule, Greater Than.

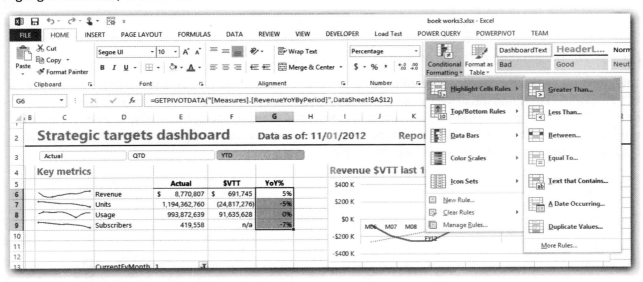

*Figure 4.72: Adding conditional formatting.*

Jim chooses to highlight all the cells that are less than zero with a subtle red color.

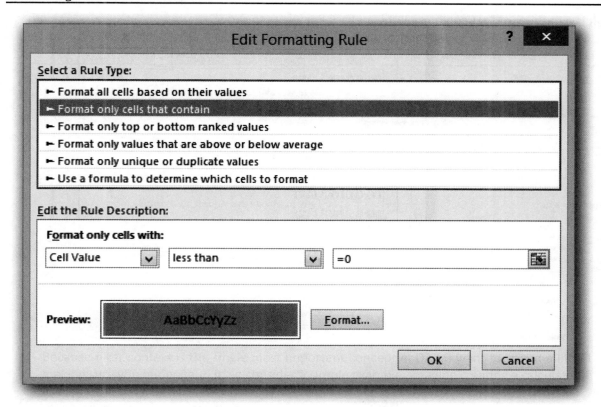

*Figure 4.73: Applying the formatting rule.*

The report now has dynamic formatting applied to cells that have a value below zero.

| Key metrics | | Actual | $VTT | YoY% |
|---|---|---|---|---|
| ⟋⟍ | Revenue | $  8,770,807 | $   691,745 | 5% |
| ⟍⟍ | Units | 1,194,362,760 | (24,817,276) | -5% |
| ⟍⟋ | Usage | 993,872,639 | 91,635,628 | 0% |
| ⟍ | Subscribers | 419,558 | n/a | -7% |

*Figure 4.74: The report with dynamic formatting applied to YoY%.*

Jim now uses the Format Painter to add the same formatting rules to all other cells in the PivotTable that contain percentages.

Jim adds the same conditional formatting rules to the other cells of the reports. Unfortunately he cannot use the Format Painter is because it would overwrite more than the conditional formatting like the format string.

The result is a dashboard that contains all the metrics Jim wants to show.

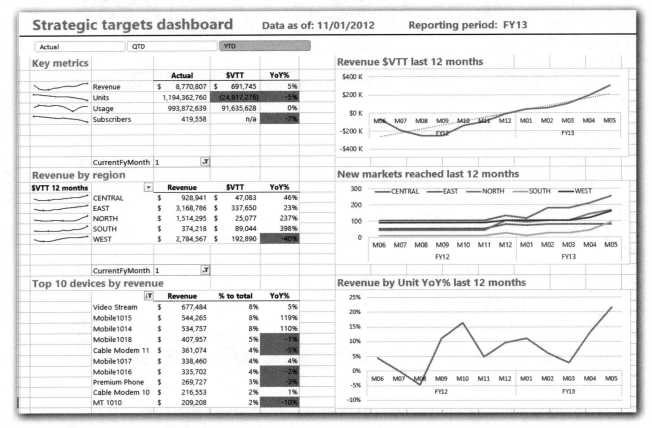

*Figure 4.75: All metrics added to the dashboard.*

## Finishing the Dashboard: The Final Checklist

Jim is now ready to finish the report and clean it up for the final view. To tidy up, he hides the items that are not needed for consuming the dashboard, such as the rows that contain the PivotTable filters. Next, from the Excel ribbon, he selects View and deselects View Formula Bar, Gridlines, and Headings. He moves the active cell to the top-left position and saves the workbook.

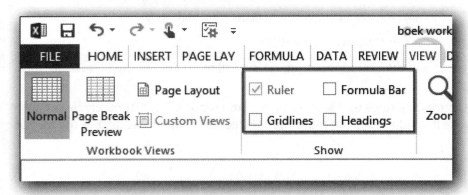

*Figure 4.76: Hiding Excel elements for the workbook.*

This results in a much cleaner version of the workbook, it's not even obvious the workbook is built in Excel:

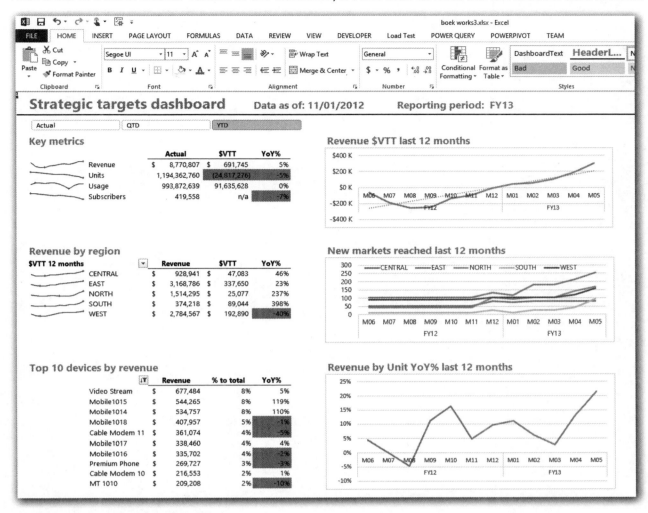

*Figure 4.77: The finished dashboard.*

It's time for Jim to do a last check of the dashboard. He considers the following questions, which control factors that make or break a dashboard:

- Are the same fonts used everywhere?
- Do the colors match up?
- Are items that belong together placed together?
- Are the items aligned properly?
- Does the data look correct?
- Do the interactive parts of the dashboard work as expected?

Now it's time for Jim to show the dashboard to some of the key users and get their feedback. The next steps is for Jim to allow his users to drill down into more details by creating detailed reports.

# 5- Building Interactive Reports with Excel and Power View

In this chapter Jim creates a detailed report in Excel that will allow users to drill into the details of the data provided in the dashboard. Jim also creates several interactive reports using Power View for Excel 2013 to allow visual data exploration.

## Building Interactive Reports with Either Excel or Power View

Jim has created a dashboard that gives only a limited high-level overview of the data. Now he wants his users to be able to drill down into more details so they can see more about what is going on.

### Creating a Revenue Report

Jim thinks he should create a detailed report on revenue. He wants users to be able to use the report to examine revenue information from several angles. They will be able to use what they find in this detailed report to answer many questions raised by the dashboard.

Jim wants to allow the users to dive into the following revenue calculations:

- Revenue by region for the current period, QTD, and YTD
- Revenue by region over the current fiscal year
- Revenue by plan type for the current period, QTD, and YTD
- Revenue by plan type over the current fiscal year
- Revenue over time
- Revenue YoY% comparison

Jim knows that this is a lot of data to show, but luckily Excel allows quite a few tricks to make this amount of data manageable.

Jim opens his Excel workbook and adds a new worksheet, which he calls Revenue. To make the report look consistent with the dashboard, he adds the same header above the report and keeps the first row and column empty. He copies the header from the DashBoard worksheet and changes the title from Strategic Targets Dashboard to Revenue Report.

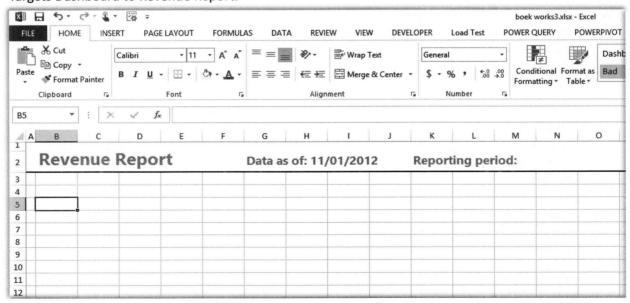

*Figure 5.1: Adding a header to a report.*

Jim wants to make this report interactive. Instead of having a static reporting period, he wants the user to choose the reporting period. He wants this report to have maximum flexibility, so he chooses to add a slicer that allows the user to select the fiscal year for which to show the data.

Jim clicks Insert, Slicer. In the Existing Connections dialog that appears, Jim selects the Data Model tab, clicks Tables in Workbook Data Model, and clicks Open.

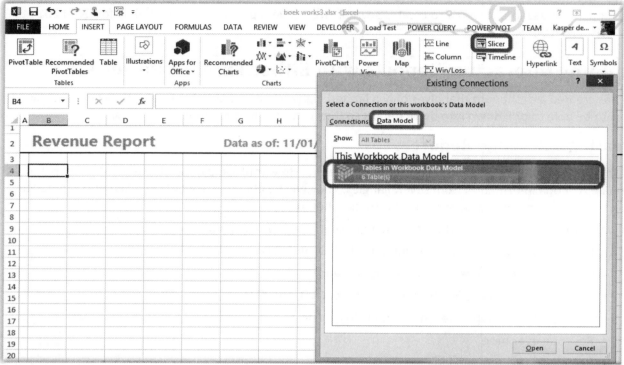

*Figure 5.2: Adding a slicer that gets data from the data model.*

The Insert Slicers dialog appears. Jim selects FyYearLabel for showing the data for that Fiscal Year.

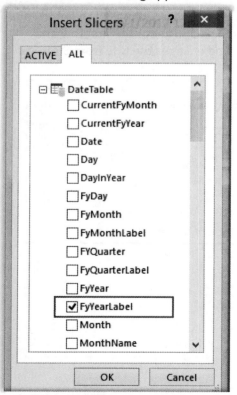

*Figure 5.3: Selecting FyYearLabel.*

Excel adds the slicer to the worksheet. Jim applies the DashboardText style to the slicer to make sure the styling in the dashboard and report is consistent.

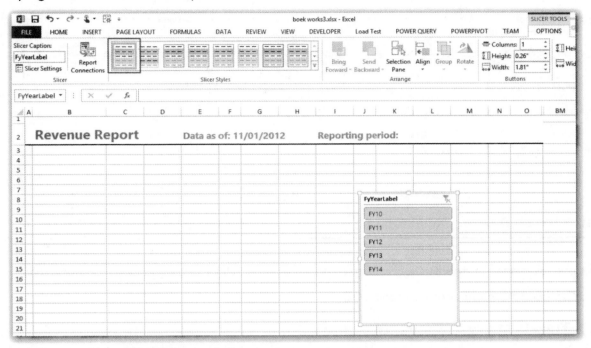

Figure 5.4: Adding a slicer to a worksheet.

Jim then selects Slicer Tools, Options, Slicer Settings. In the Slicer Settings dialog that appears, he deselects Display Header.

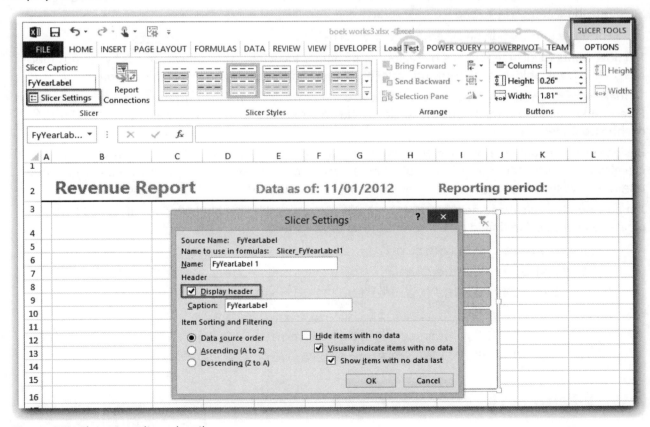

Figure 5.5: Changing slicer details.

Jim then drags the slicers up next to Reporting Period in the header and sets the number of columns to 5. This gives him the view he wants for this slicer.

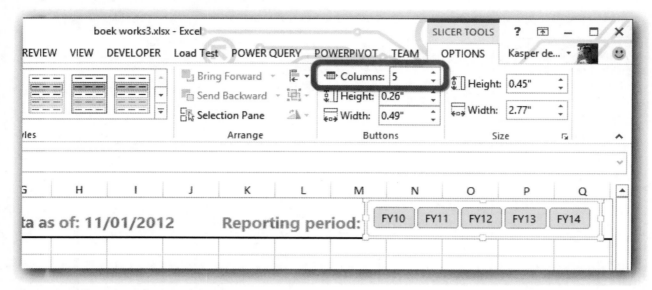

*Figure 5.6: Changing the number of slicer columns.*

### Excel Tip: Slicers

Slicers, which were introduced in Excel 2010, are easy-to-use filtering components. A slicer contains a set of buttons that enable you to quickly filter the data in a PivotTable (or PivotChart) report without the need to open drop-down lists to find the items you want to filter. You can use slicers in any Excel PivotTable, whether it uses the Excel data model or native PivotTables. Slicers provide a great way to show data interactively.

For more information on slicers, see this Excel help topic: http://ppivot.us/Hx3EX.

Jim now wants to include revenue by region, so he adds a PivotTable that shows regions by various metrics. In this PivotTable, he also turns off AutoFit Columns on Update in the PivotTable options.

To make sure he shows only the sales for the current month, Jim drags the CurrentFyMonth field under Filters and selects 1. He then adds the Regions field under Rows and the Period field he created for the dashboard under Columns.

Besides using the date period table we created in chapter 4 as a slicer, as he did for the dashboard, Jim can also use it as a header on a PivotTable. Jim can use it to show revenue, revenue target, variance from target, and year-over-year growth for the values in the Period column: Actual, QTD, and YTD.

Jim now needs a calculated field for revenue target. He copies the RevenuebyPeriod calculated field and creates a new calculated field called RevenueToTargetbyPeriod:

```
[RevenueTargetByPeriod] =
IF([isReportSlicerSet],
    SWITCH(VALUES(varPeriod[Period]) ,
        "Actual",[Sum of Revenuetarget],
        "YTD",[Sum of RevenueTarget F QTD],
        "QTD",[Sum of RevenueTarget F QTD]
        )
    )
```

Figure 5.7 shows how the PivotTable looks at this point. It shows each calculation for each time period, for each region along with the grand total.

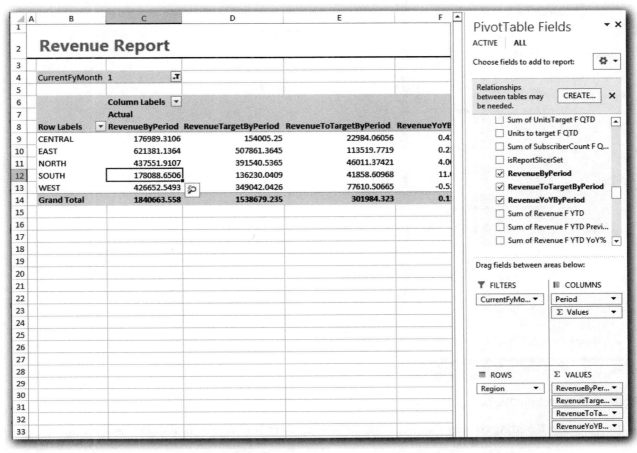

*Figure 5.7: Adding values to the PivotTable.*

Because it's hard to see the entire table, Jim wants to apply some formatting. He starts by renaming the calculated fields to be more user friendly. Jim goes to the Values area in the PivotTable, clicks the Revenue-byPeriod calculated field, and selects Value Field Settings.

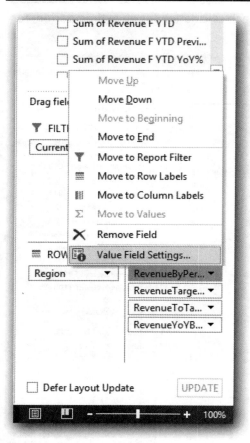

*Figure 5.8: Selecting "Value field settings"*

In the Value Field Settings dialog that appears, Jim sets Custom Name to Actual.Value fieldsettings

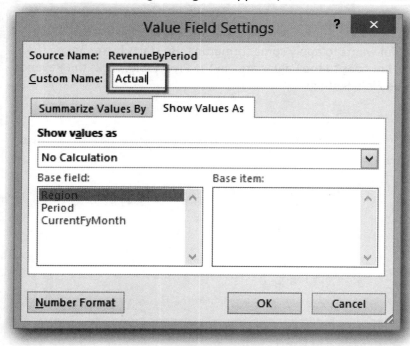

*Figure 5.9: Changing the name of the field*

Then he renames all the other calculated fields under Values, using the same method:

- He uses the name Target for RevenueTargetByPeriod.
- He uses the name $VTT for RevenueToTargetByPeriod.
- He uses the name YoY% for RevenueYoYByPeriod.

To give the PivotTable a clean and tidy look, he applies 10-point Segoe UI font to the PivotTable and selects Design, None on the PivotTable tools tab. The PivotTable is much easier to read already.

| Row Labels | Actual | Target | $VTT | YOY% | Actual | Target | $VTT | YOY% | Actual | Target | $VTT | YOY% |
|---|---|---|---|---|---|---|---|---|---|---|---|---|
| | | | | | QTD | | | | YTD | | | |
| CENTRAL | 176989.3106 | 154005.25 | 22984.06056 | 0.426441191 | 376493.8258 | 339634.8069 | 36859.0189 | 0.474847977 | 928941.3895 | 339634.8069 | 47083.24622 | 0.459961229 |
| EAST | 621381.1364 | 507861.3645 | 113519.7719 | 0.235091473 | 1338123.847 | 1132024.174 | 206099.673 | 0.301100451 | 3168785.855 | 1132024.174 | 337649.974 | 0.234202283 |
| NORTH | 437551.9107 | 391540.5365 | 46011.37421 | 4.004510035 | 792710.9118 | 726566.61 | 66144.3018 | 3.417166652 | 1514294.655 | 726566.61 | 25077.29482 | 2.370939063 |
| SOUTH | 178088.6506 | 136230.0409 | 41858.60968 | 11.06866352 | 256821.1478 | 191890.191 | 64930.95682 | 7.561438499 | 374218.1007 | 191890.191 | 89044.36484 | 3.980742021 |
| WEST | 426652.5493 | 349042.0426 | 77610.50665 | -0.522804344 | 893938.1411 | 776118.3689 | 117819.7722 | -0.512963843 | 2784567.119 | 776118.3689 | 192890.153 | -0.399906664 |
| Grand Total | 1840663.558 | 1538679.235 | 301984.323 | 0.133794883 | 3658087.874 | 3166234.151 | 491853.7227 | 0.098968336 | 8770807.118 | 3166234.151 | 691745.0329 | 0.048095047 |

*Figure 5.10: Styling the PivotTable.*

Because the numbers are not formatted, Jim decides to change all columns that contain revenue to currency style without decimal places and YoY% columns to percentage style, using the Number field on the Home tab.

To accentuate the header of the PivotTable, Jim selects the header, sets the background color to light gray, and centers the text in the cell. Jim notices that the columns are way too wide, so he selects all columns from the PivotTable, right-clicks, and select Column Width. He then experiments and finds 9 to be the optimal width. Finally, he removes the text Row Labels from the PivotTable because it doesn't provide any value.

| | Actual | Target | $VTT | YOY% | Actual | Target | $VTT | YOY% | Actual | Target | $VTT | YOY% |
|---|---|---|---|---|---|---|---|---|---|---|---|---|
| | | | | | QTD | | | | YTD | | | |
| CENTRAL | $176,989 | $154,005 | $22,984 | 43% | $376,494 | $339,635 | $36,859 | 47% | $928,941 | $339,635 | $47,083 | 46% |
| EAST | $621,381 | $507,861 | $113,520 | 24% | $1,338,124 | $1,132,024 | $206,100 | 30% | $3,168,786 | $1,132,024 | $337,650 | 23% |
| NORTH | $437,552 | $391,541 | $46,011 | 400% | $792,711 | $726,567 | $66,144 | 342% | $1,514,295 | $726,567 | $25,077 | 237% |
| SOUTH | $178,089 | $136,230 | $41,859 | 1107% | $256,821 | $191,890 | $64,931 | 756% | $374,218 | $191,890 | $89,044 | 398% |
| WEST | $426,653 | $349,042 | $77,611 | -52% | $893,938 | $776,118 | $117,820 | -51% | $2,784,567 | $776,118 | $192,890 | -40% |
| Grand Total | $1,840,664 | $1,538,679 | $301,984 | 13% | $3,658,088 | $3,166,234 | $491,854 | 10% | $8,770,807 | $3,166,234 | $691,745 | 5% |

*Figure 5.11: Styling the PivotTable better.*

Jim is pretty happy with the PivotTable now, but he notices one important thing: The slicer is not connected. He needs to be able to show information for each fiscal year. To connect the slicer, he selects PivotTable Tools, Analyze, Filter Connections, FyYearLabel.

Now Jim realizes he made a mistake. Because he selected the CurrentFyMonth column as a filter, selecting any other fiscal year will not work because CurrentFyMonth is bound to the current fiscal year rather than to each fiscal year. He needs to find a different way to set this filter on the PivotTable, so he decides to add a new calculated column that selects the last month for each year.

Jim opens Power Pivot and goes to the DateTable table. Jim wants to be able to select the last date for each year, so he creates a calculated field for this:

```
[Last fiscal month of the year] =
    CALCULATE(
        LASTNONBLANK(DateTable[Date]
                        ,[Sum of Revenue])
        ,ALLEXCEPT(DateTable
                        ,DateTable[FyYear])
        )
```

Finally, he removes the row label header "Row Labels" from the PivotTable because it doesn't provide any value. Jim selects the cell and just replaces the text "Row Labels" with a space.

> This expression gets the last value for the Date column in the DateTable table for each fiscal year for which that date has revenue. Instead of using the `ALL` function, which would get the last value for the entire table, this expression uses the `ALLEXCEPT` function. The `ALLEXCEPT` function removes all filters in the table except for the columns supplied in the arguments. In this case, it will always give Jim the last period for the entire year; it will override months, weeks, and days but not years.

To test the new calculated field, Jim puts it into a PivotTable with FyYear under Rows. Jim knows that the calculated field works because he can see the last date in each year.

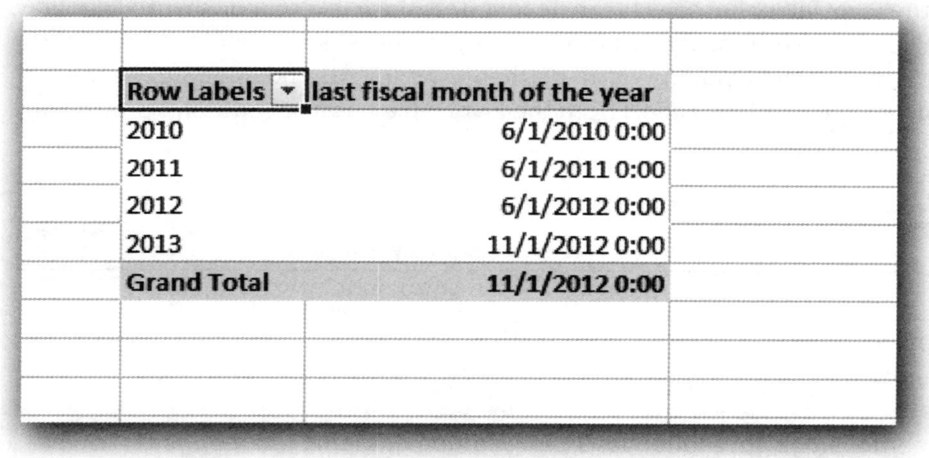

| Row Labels ▼ | last fiscal month of the year |
|---|---|
| 2010 | 6/1/2010 0:00 |
| 2011 | 6/1/2011 0:00 |
| 2012 | 6/1/2012 0:00 |
| 2013 | 11/1/2012 0:00 |
| Grand Total | 11/1/2012 0:00 |

Figure 5.12: Testing the calculated field.

Jim now wants to create a calculated column in the DateTable table so he can filter on it in his PivotTables. He adds the following calculated column to the DateTable table:

```
[LastFyMonthofYear] =
    IF(
        [Year]=YEAR([Last fiscal month of the year])
        &&
        [Month]=MONTH([Last fiscal month of the year])
        ,1
        ,0
        )
```

> This formula executes for each row in the table, comparing the year of the current row in the DateTable table with the result of the calculated field.

Jim wants to test his calculated column again, so he updates his PivotTable and adds FyMonthLabel under FyYear on Rows and the new calculated column LastFyMonthofYear under Filters. He then sees that his calculated columns works.

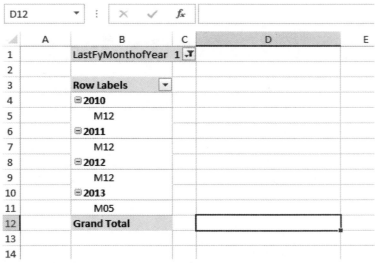

Figure 5.13: Testing the calculated column.

Jim decides he no longer needs the "Last fiscal month of the year" calculated field for direct use in his PivotTables, so he hides it in the calculated field grid in the Power Pivot window. He also removes the worksheet that he added to test his calculations.

Jim now updates his Revenue table to use the new calculated field and tests whether the PivotTable now works when he changes the fiscal year with the slicer. He is happy to see that it does.

Now that the fiscal year slicer works, Jim wants to allow the users to slice and dice on other dimensions. He wants them to be able to see numbers by region and state and by device and plan type. Jim plans to use slicers for this. He starts by adding a slicer for region and state by selecting Insert, Slicers. In the Insert Slicers dialog that appears, he selects Region and StateShort.

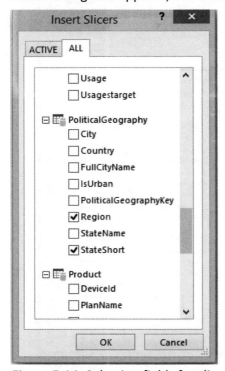

Figure 5.14: Selecting fields for slicers.

Excel adds the slicers to the middle of the workbook. Jim moves them to the region above the PivotTable, making sure the slicers don't overlap with the PivotTable filters because he wants to hide these rows later on. He also makes sure to select the DashboardText style so these new slicers look like the first one.

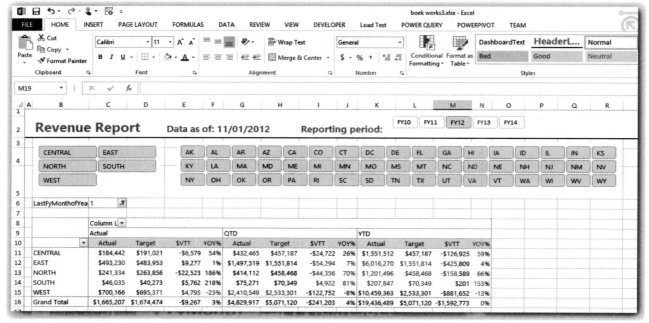

*Figure 5.15: Adding region and state slicers.*

Jim creates device type and plan type slicers, which he adds to the right of the PivotTable. He creates a new style for them to show that these slicers are a different type. He selects subtle colors that look distinct from but consistent with the other slicers.

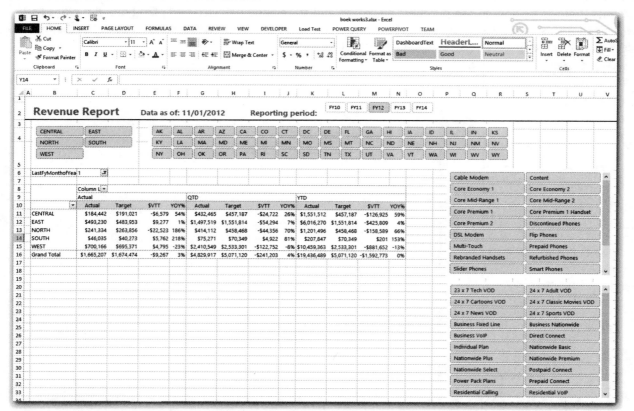

*Figure 5.16: Adding plan type and device type slicers.*

> You might notice that this report isn't designed the same way as the dashboard. The idea is that a user can choose to go to a report to see details and really dive into the subject area. The goal is not for the user to be in and out in a minute, as with a dashboard. Still, some of the same rules apply to these reports as to dashboards, like making sure you don't put attention where it is not needed, and align objects appropriately.

Now Jim connects all the slicers to the PivotTable and tests whether they work as expected. They do. Jim wants to make sure the numbers pop on the report, so he adds some conditional formatting to the report. He selects each Actual column in his PivotTable and then selects Home, Conditional Formatting, Data Bars.

| | Actual | | | | QTD | | | | YTD | | | |
|---|---|---|---|---|---|---|---|---|---|---|---|---|
| | Actual | Target | $VTT | YOY% | Actual | Target | $VTT | YOY% | Actual | Target | $VTT | YOY% |
| CENTRAL | $184,442 | $191,021 | -$6,579 | 54% | $432,465 | $457,187 | -$24,722 | 26% | $1,551,512 | $457,187 | -$126,925 | 59% |
| EAST | $493,230 | $483,953 | $9,277 | 1% | $1,497,519 | $1,551,814 | -$54,294 | 7% | $6,015,270 | $1,551,814 | -$425,809 | 4% |
| NORTH | $241,334 | $263,856 | -$22,523 | 186% | $414,112 | $458,468 | -$44,356 | 70% | $1,201,496 | $458,468 | -$158,589 | 66% |
| SOUTH | $46,035 | $40,273 | $5,762 | 218% | $75,271 | $70,349 | $4,922 | 81% | $207,847 | $70,349 | $201 | 153% |
| WEST | $700,166 | $695,371 | $4,795 | -23% | $2,410,549 | $2,533,301 | -$122,752 | -8% | $10,459,363 | $2,533,301 | -$881,652 | -13% |
| Grand Total | $1,665,207 | $1,674,474 | -$9,267 | 3% | $4,829,917 | $5,071,120 | -$241,203 | 4% | $19,436,489 | $5,071,120 | -$1,592,773 | 0% |

*Figure 5.17: Adding data bars to the PivotTable.*

In addition to showing the last month of the selected fiscal year, Jim wants to show the revenue for all the months for the selected fiscal year. He wants to put a PivotTable for this right next to the PivotTable that show the values for the current month, and he wants to use the existing PivotTable as a template. He selects the PivotTable and then selects PivotTable Tools, Analyze, Entire PivotTable. He then copies and pastes the entire PivotTable right next to the original PivotTable so he has a complete copy of the Pivot-Table, including all the styling and connected slicers. He then adds FyMonthLabel under Rows, removes LastFyMonthofYear from under Filters, and moves the Period column from under Rows to under Filters to make sure he shows only the actual values for each month. He can now see the revenue for each month for the selected fiscal year.

| Period | Actual | | | | | | | | | | | | | | | |
|---|---|---|---|---|---|---|---|---|---|---|---|---|---|---|---|---|
| | M01 | | | | M02 | | | | M03 | | | | M04 | | | |
| | Actual | Target | $VTT | YOY% | Actual | Target | $VTT | YOY% | Actual | Target | $VTT | YOY% | Actual | Target | $VTT | YO |
| CENTRAL | $120,851 | $135,815 | -$14,963 | 152 % | $123,897 | $135,972 | -$12,075 | 159 % | $136,254 | $137,247 | -$993 | 183 % | $131,199 | $137,173 | -$5,975 | |
| EAST | $488,795 | $547,770 | -$58,975 | -1 % | $503,926 | $547,671 | -$43,745 | 2 % | $546,300 | $544,273 | $2,027 | 11 % | $525,350 | $543,939 | -$18,589 | |
| NORTH | $85,589 | $101,727 | -$16,139 | 119 % | $88,466 | $101,275 | -$12,810 | 129 % | $95,704 | $99,648 | -$3,943 | 146 % | $92,030 | $100,452 | -$8,422 | |
| SOUTH | $14,394 | $15,269 | -$876 | | $14,727 | $14,992 | -$265 | | $16,015 | $15,316 | $700 | | $15,241 | $14,946 | $295 | |
| WEST | $899,684 | $1,019,155 | -$119,471 | -20 % | $917,900 | $1,004,481 | -$86,581 | -18 % | $987,174 | $991,890 | -$4,716 | -11 % | $941,383 | $983,019 | -$41,636 | |
| Grand Tot | $1,609,313 | $1,819,736 | -$210,423 | -6 % | $1,648,916 | $1,804,391 | -$155,476 | -3 % | $1,781,447 | $1,788,372 | -$6,925 | 5 % | $1,705,203 | $1,779,529 | -$74,327 | |

*Figure 5.18: A PivotTable showing revenue for all months of the year.*

Through all his changes, Jim has added a lot of data to the sheet. Most users won't want to see all of it all the time, so Jim needs to figure out how to show only the appropriate information when needed. He starts by hiding the rows that contain the PivotTable filters. Jim thinks not all the users need to see the revenue for all months, and he knows he can hide this view by default by using the Excel Group function.

### Excel Tip: Grouping (Outlining) Data

Excel has a neat trick that I learned about recently while working with some great Excel professionals who work at Microsoft as analysts. The Group function in Excel allows you to collapse and expand a group of columns or rows with one click of the button. This enables you to provide a lot of data in a without having it visible all the time. For more information, see http://ppivot.us/9DB3V.

Jim moves the plan type and device type slicers to the right of the copied PivotTable (the columns that he wants the user to be able to collapse). He selects all the columns the PivotTable contains and then selects Data, Group.

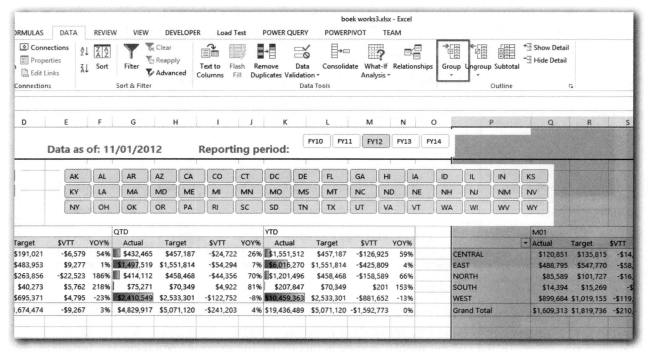

*Figure 5.19: Grouping a range of cells together.*

Jim now closes the group by clicking the – sign in the outline of the worksheet that showed up after creating the groups. Now the entire PivotTable is hidden.

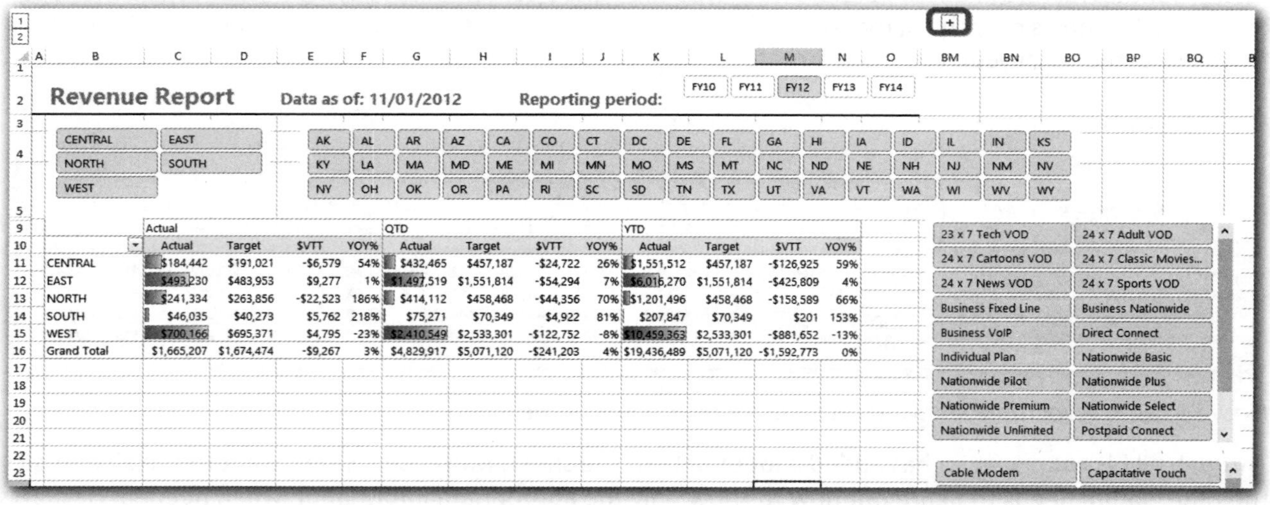

*Figure 5.20: Grouped the columns together in a single outline.*

Jim also wants the user to be able to close the regions, so he selects the regions and groups them as well. He renames the grand total to By Region to make it easy to see where to open and close the details.

To add the same view for plan type, Jim copies both PivotTables a few rows below the original PivotTables and replaces Region with PlanType.

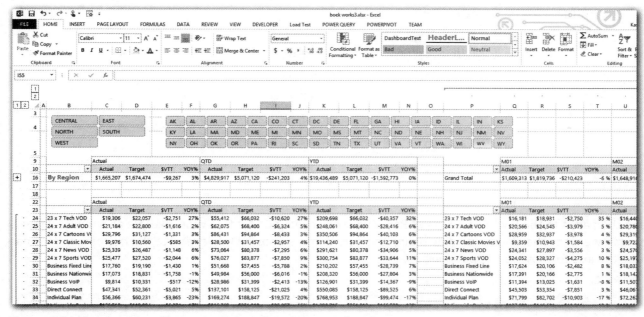

*Figure 5.21: Revenue by plan type, with a closed group of regions.*

# Creating a Chart of Revenue over Time

Jim wants the report to show another aspect of revenue: revenue over time. He decides to create a comparison chart that shows revenue for the current year, revenue one year ago, and revenue two years ago.

He inserts a PivotChart below the PivotTable with one row in between by pressing the Alt key and dragging the chart with the mouse. Then he connects the fiscal year slicer to the PivotChart.

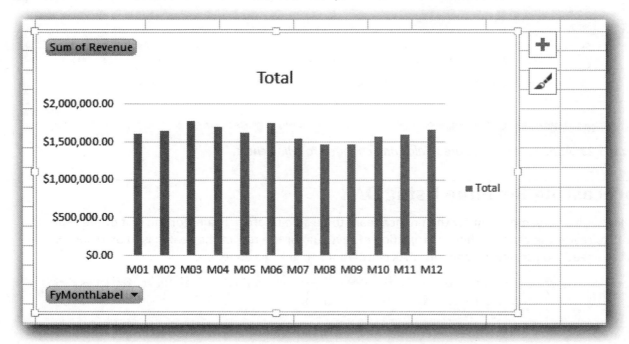

*Figure 5.22: Inserting a PivotChart with Sum of Revenue by FyMonthLabel*

Jim changes the chart type to line chart. He wants to add Sum of Revenue PreviousYear, but he is unable to find the calculated field for this. He then remembers that he hid this calculated field earlier, so he goes back to the calculation area in the Power Pivot window and unhides the calculated field. He then copies this calculated field to allow calculation of the sum of revenue two years ago:

```
[Sum of Revenue Two Year] =
    IF(
            HASONEVALUE(DateTable[FyYear])
                ,CALCULATE([Sum of Revenue]
                    ,DATEADD(DateTable[Date]
                            ,-2
                            ,YEAR
                        )
                    )
        )
```

Jim then adds to the PivotChart Sum of Revenue for last year and for two years ago. He also makes a few visual tweaks to the chart, including hiding the field buttons, moving the legend to the bottom, and formatting the axis to show values per millions.

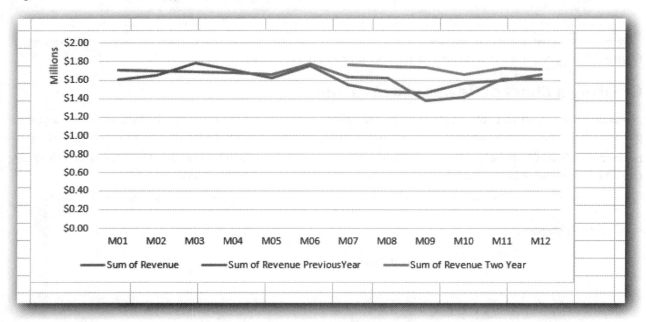

*Figure 5.23: Added more calculated fields and changed to a line chart.*

# Forecasting Revenue Using DAX

Jim knows it's very important for the finance team to be able to project sales for the rest of the year. He wants to revise the chart to show a projection of revenue for the rest of the year, based on results in the past. He needs to use several complex DAX calculations to get this done.

> Don't be too overwhelmed by the DAX expressions in this chapter, these examples show you what the DAX language is capable of.

The first thing Jim wants to do is determine the growth rate that he wants to use to project the future sales. He wants to use the average year-over-year growth rate for the past six months to project into the future. He uses the following DAX calculations to accomplish this:

```
[Avg GrowthRate last 6 months]=
CALCULATE(
            AVERAGEX(
                        VALUES(DateTable[YearMonth])
                        ,[Sum of Revenue YoY%])
                ,ALL(DateTable)
                ,DATESINPERIOD(DateTable[Date]
                        ,CALCULATE(
                                LASTNONBLANK(DateTable[Date]
                                        ,[Sum of Revenue])
                                ,ALL(DateTable))
                        ,-6
                        ,MONTH)
            )
```

> This calculated field determines the average of [Sum of Revenue YoY%] for each DateTable[YearMonth] for which the dates fall within the period up to six months before the last date in which there is [Sum of Revenue].
>
> The AVERAGEX function ensures that the average is calculating the [Sum of Revenue YoY%] values for each DateTable[YearMonth] value. The CALCULATE function allows the calculation to reach outside the current date context determined by the PivotChart by using ALL(DateTable). Then the DATESINPERIOD function adds a new context. This function returns all rows for the DateTable[Date] column between the LASTNONBLANK DateTable[Date] value where there is a [Sum of Revenue] and six months previous to that date, making sure to use the entire DateTable table by using CALCULATE and the ALL(DateTable) filter.

Next, Jim creates a calculated field that determines the number of months since the current month. This will allow him to multiply the average growth rate by the months in the future. The more months in the future the higher the number.

```
[MonthsSinceCurrentMonth] =
    (
        YEAR(STARTOFMONTH(DateTable[Date]))
        -
        YEAR([Absolute Last Invoice Date])
    ) * 12
    +
    MONTH(STARTOFMONTH(DateTable[Date]))
    -
    MONTH([Absolute Last Invoice Date])
```

This function calculates the YEAR of the first day of the month, using STAR-TOFMONTH for the current DateTable[Date] column then subtracting the YEAR of the date returned by the [Absolute Last Invoice Date]. The result is multiplied by 12 because each year has 12 months. The results are then added to the difference between the MONTH returned by the STARTOFMONTH function for the current DateTable[Date] and MONTH of the date returned by the [Absolute Last Invoice Date]. This results in the difference in months between two dates.

For more information on these types of expressions, see http://ppivot.us/Zz1zb.

Jim wants to use the two previous calculations to determine the projected growth. He uses the POWER function to raise 1 plus the average growth rate by the number of months since the current month. This gives a nice trajectory for the revenue growth:

```
[ProjectedGrowthFactor] =
    POWER(1 + [Avg GrowthRate last 6 months]
        ,[MonthsSinceCurrentMonth])
```

For a similar calculation, see this blog post on PowerPivotPro.com: http://ppivot.us/CBiYi.

Now all that needs to be done is to multiply the revenue from the last month by the projected growth factor. Jim determines the Last Revenue value for Contoso:

```
[Last Revenue] =
    CALCULATE([Sum of Revenue]
        ,DateTable[CurrentFyMonth]=1
        ,ALL(DateTable)
        )
```

This calculated field uses the ALL function to determine [Sum of Revenue] where CurrentFyMonth is 1 for the entire DateTable table.

Finally, Jim can multiply [Last Revenue] by [ProjectedGrowthFactor], but only if [MonthsSinceCurrentMonth] returns a positive number, meaning a month is in the future. He adds this calculated field to the chart and changes the projected line from a solid line to a dotted line:

```
[ProjectedRevenue] =
    IF([MonthsSinceCurrentMonth] >= 0
        ,[Last Revenue] * [ProjectedGrowthFactor])
```

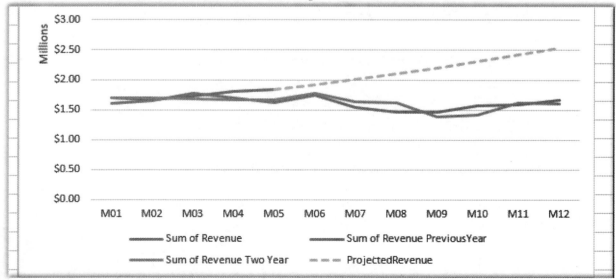

*Figure 5.24: Adding projected revenue to the chart.*

While testing this calculated field, Jim thinks it would be great if he could make the calculated field determine the average growth rate, based on a number of months that the user can select. Jim wants to add a slicer above the chart where the user can select the months to use in the forecast. He therefore adds a table to his previously created variables worksheet, with the values 3, 6, 9, 12, and 24. He then adds this table to the data model.

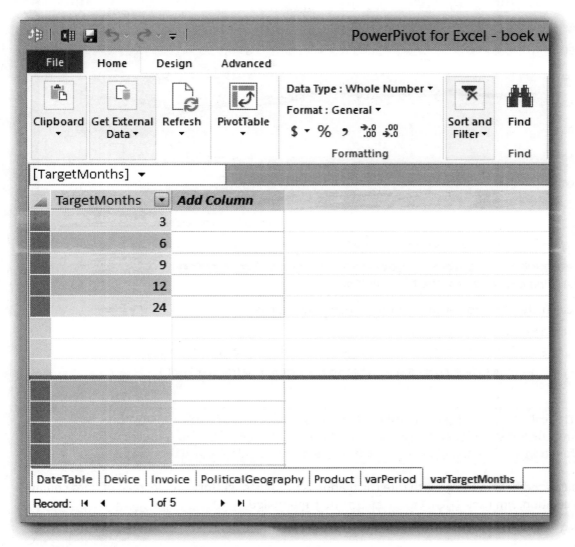

*Figure 5.25: Adding an Excel table to the data model.*

Jim uses this table in the model to add a slicer above the PivotChart and connects the slicer. He also adds a title to the chart.

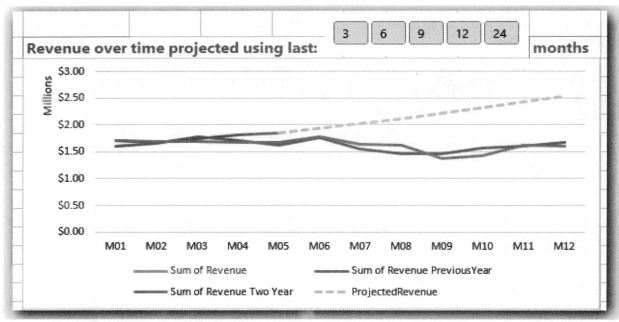

*Figure 5.26: Adding a slicer and a title to a PivotChart.*

Jim needs a calculated field to get the months selected by the user:

```
[getTargetMonths] =
    IF(HASONEVALUE(varTargetMonths[TargetMonths])
        ,VALUES(varTargetMonths[TargetMonths])
        ,12)
```

> This calculated field gets the value of `varTargetMonths[TargetMonths]` for the current slicer when there is only one value, determined by the `HASONEVALUE` function. If more than one values are selected, the calculated field returns `12`.

Using this calculated field in the growth rate calculation is pretty straightforward. Instead of hard coding `-6` in the calculation, Jim uses `[getTargetMonths]` multiplied by `-1`:

```
[Avg GrowthRate last 6 months]=
CALCULATE(
        AVERAGEX(
                VALUES(DateTable[YearMonth])
                ,[Sum of Revenue YoY%])
        ,ALL(DateTable)
        ,DATESINPERIOD(DateTable[Date]
            ,CALCULATE(
                    LASTNONBLANK(DateTable[Date]
                            ,[Sum of Revenue])
                    ,ALL(DateTable))
            , [getTargetMonths] * -1
            ,MONTH)
        )
```

This calculation allows users to play with the slicer to show the projected growth per month.

## Comparing Year-over-Year Growth

The last chart Jim wants to add is a visualization that makes it possible to compare year-over-year growth for the revenue to the number of units and usage to see what the relationships are. Jim adds a PivotChart to the report and connects all the slicers to the PivotChart. He then adds FyMonthLabel under Rows and adds Sum of Revenue YoY%, Sum of Usage YoY%, and Sum of Units YoY% under Values.

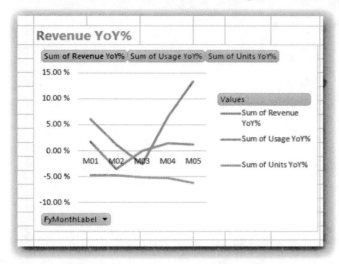

*Figure 5.27: Comparing growth rates for several years in one chart.*

Next, Jim hides the field buttons and moves the legend down to the bottom. The report now allows users to dive into revenue from several angles. Jim finishes up the report by hiding the gridlines, headings, and formula bar again.

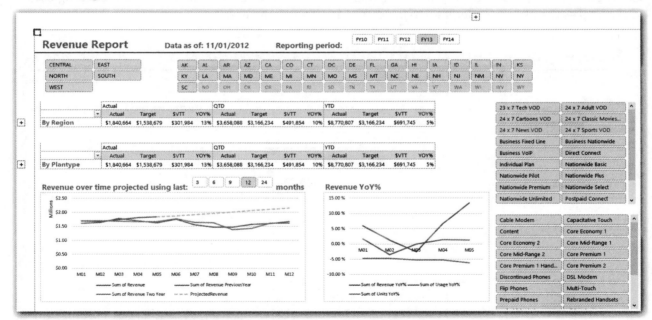

*Figure 5.28: A finished revenue report.*

## Creating Links Between the Worksheets

Jim wants users to be able to go from the dashboard directly to the Revenue report. To do this, he uses the Excel hyperlink function: He selects the Revenue by Region header and then selects Insert, Hyperlink. In the Edit Hyperlink dialog, Jim chooses the Revenue worksheet as the place in the document to which a click brings a user.

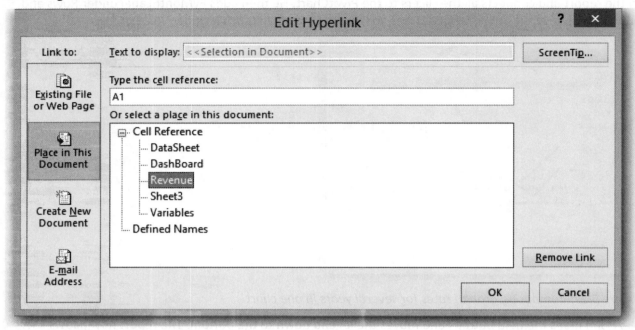

*Figure 5.29: Creating hyperlinks.*

Adding the hyperlink resets the styling of the title, so Jim uses the Format Painter to add the styling back. He also makes the header underlined to indicate that it's a link the user can click.

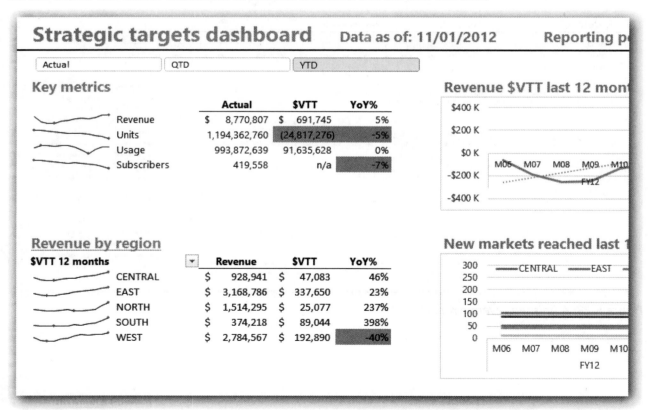

*Figure 5.30: A linked header.*

# Using Power View for Data Exploration

Jim wants his users to be able to work with the data he collected for the dashboard more interactively. He decides to use a new feature of Excel 2013 called Power View to create interactive insights about revenue by region and product revenue.

### Power View Tip: What Is Power View?

Power View is an exciting product that came out of the same SQL Server BI team that delivered Power Pivot. It provides a highly interactive data exploration, visualization, and presentation experience that encourages intuitive ad hoc reporting. Power View, together with the Excel data model, makes it easier to create beautiful and insightful reports that can help tell a story. For example, when presenting a financial report to a group of users, you can use Power View to create a great-looking report that is highly interactive.

Several features set Power View apart from Excel and traditional reporting tools:

- It has the ability to visualize data with no more than two clicks.
- It is very simple and intuitive to use.
- It provides a high level of interactivity between the elements on a sheet, allowing users to gain new insight without having to leave the worksheet.
- It allows you to create new visualizations, such as a play axis, maps, cards, and images.
- It allows user to cycle through the different types of visualizations quickly.

Power View is available in three flavors:

- **Power View for SharePoint:** This is a web version of Power View that comes as part of SharePoint. It allows you to create reports in a browser on top of Power Pivot workbooks or on external Analysis Services models. This first version of Power View initially shipped with SQL Server 2012.

- **Power View for Office 365:** This is the same web version that ships with SharePoint. In it, the reports are embedded inside an Excel workbook that is shared to Office 365. This "cloud" version of Power View will be updated more regularly than the first one.

- **Power View for Excel 2013:** This version of Power View ships as part of Excel 2013. The new Power View worksheet type allows users to create Power View reports based on the Excel data model or on external Analysis Services models.

## Using Maps to Visualize Regional Sales

To insert a Power View worksheet into his Excel workbook, Jim selects Insert, Power View.

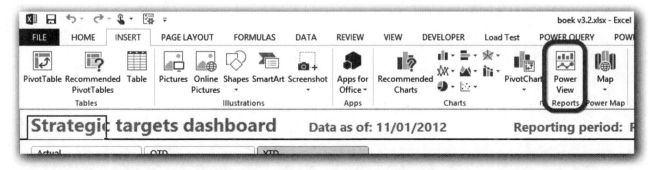

*Figure 5.31: Inserting a Power View worksheet.*

### Power View Tip: Where Is My Power Pivot or Power View?

Some versions of Excel 2013 do not have Power Pivot or Power View. Power Pivot and Power View are available only in certain SKUs. For more, see this blog post: http://ppivot.us/YzsJJ.

This adds a new Power View worksheet to the workbook

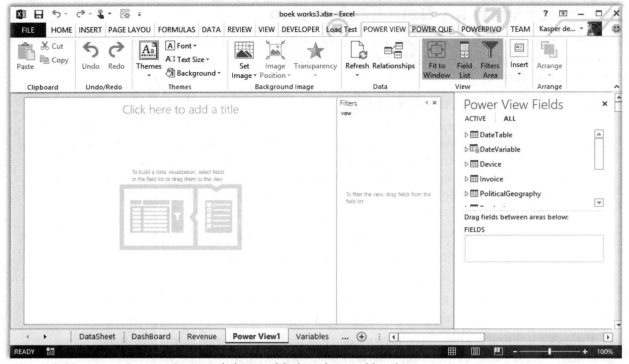

*Figure 5.32: A new Power View worksheet added to the workbook.*

## Power View Tip: Getting Stated with Power View

Working with Power View is very different from working with Excel. Some differences are immediately visible, such as Power View having no grid and having a pane open on the right.

*Figure 5.33: Taking a look at the Power View canvas.*

Instead of adding charts directly to the Excel canvas, Power View has a freeform canvas that doesn't have the restriction of gridlines. (No more messing up alignment because you inserted a new row!) You start creating a new visualization by selecting a field from the field list; Power View adds the field to the field well and adds a visualization in the main canvas, in the first available free spot. As mentioned earlier, this is a freeform canvas, so you can drag the visualization to anyplace on the canvas.

Another difference between Power View and Excel is that the canvas is limited to one screen, and you cannot scroll outside it. The main Power View canvas always uses an aspect ratio of 4:3. In Power View, it is also possible to add filters to all the visualizations on a worksheet by adding a filter to the Filters area. This area consists of two parts: a View tab and a Chart area. Filters added to the View tab are applied to the entire worksheet, and filters added to the Chart tab are applied to just the currently selected visualization.

To add a title, Jim selects the title bar on top of the worksheet, types Revenue by Region, and aligns the title to the left by using the alignment control on the Power View text tab.

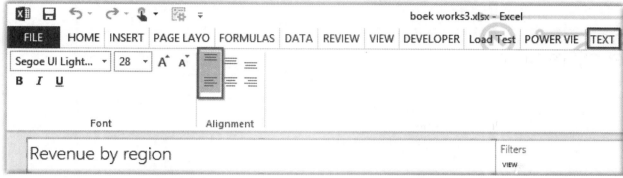

*Figure 5.34: Changing text settings.*

Jim doesn't plan to add any filters right now, so he clicks the Filters Area button on the Power View tab to close the Filters area. This gives him more room to work on the report because the main Power View canvas automatically scales to maximize the space available in Excel.

Jim wants to show the year-to-date variance to target by region. He selects the Region field to add a table with all the regions to the canvas.

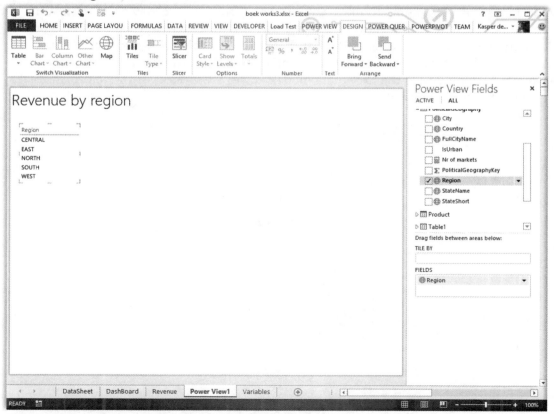

*Figure 5.35: A table added to the Power View canvas.*

Jim then selects the Revenue to Target F YTD calculated field to add it to the table. This calculated field won't return any results because there is no fiscal year selected. Jim wants to resolve this, so he clicks outside the current table on the canvas to remove the selection from the current table.

Now he opens the DateTable table in the field list and selects the FyYearLabel check box. Power View adds a new table to the canvas. Jim wants to use the table values as a slicer, so he selects Design, Slicer.

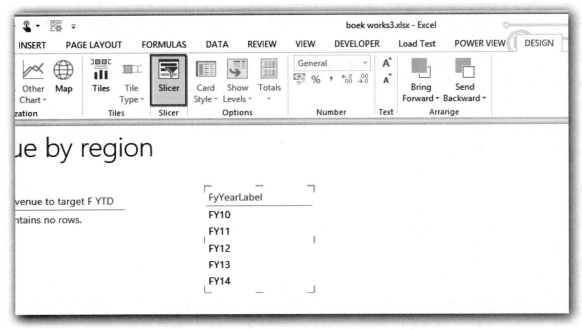

*Figure 5.36: Creating a slicer from a table.*

### Power View Tip: Setting the Format of a Calculated Field in Power View

It's very important to use formatting to make your visualizations more readable. In Excel, you can use Excel formatting to format a chart or table any way you want. In Power View, formatting works a bit differently: Power View uses the format that is set on a column or calculated field in the Excel data model. When you set or change a format in the Power Pivot window, information about that format is stored inside the Excel data model. Power View retrieves this information and it then applies the correct formatting.

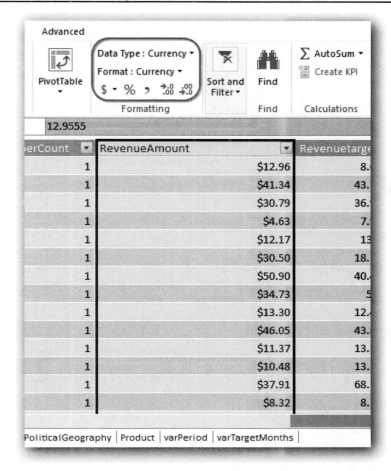

*Figure 5.37: Changing the format of a column or calculated field.*

Power View changes the table into a slicer, and Jim selects FY13. Now the values show up in the previously added table.

Revenue by region

| Region | Revenue to target F YTD | FyYearLabel |
|--------|-------------------------|-------------|
| CENTRAL | 47,083.25 | FY10 |
| EAST | 337,649.97 | FY11 |
| NORTH | 25,077.29 | FY12 |
| SOUTH | 89,044.36 | ▪ FY13 |
| WEST | 192,890.15 | FY14 |
| **Total** | **691,745.03** | |

*Figure 5.38: A slicer and a table on the Power View canvas.*

To visualize the variance to target by region, Jim decides to switch to a column bar chart. He moves the chart to the top-right corner and changes the default sort from region to variance to target by hovering over the chart and selecting the sort options.

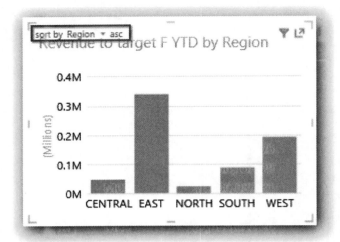

*Figure 5.39: Changing the sort options for a chart in Power View.*

Jim also wants to add his own label to the chart, so he turns off the one provided by Power View in the Layout tab.

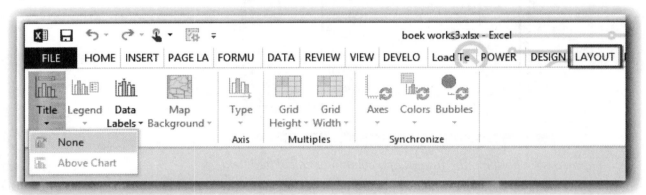

*Figure 5.40: Removing the chart title.*

One of the great visualizations Power View offers that Excel doesn't is a map chart. Jim decides to add this chart to visualize the sales per region. He adds both StateShort and Sum of Revenue to the canvas and selects Design, Map. He then drags the visualization next to the previous chart and drags the Fiscal Year slicer on top of the map. (Power View allows charts to overlap.) This gives him a good start.

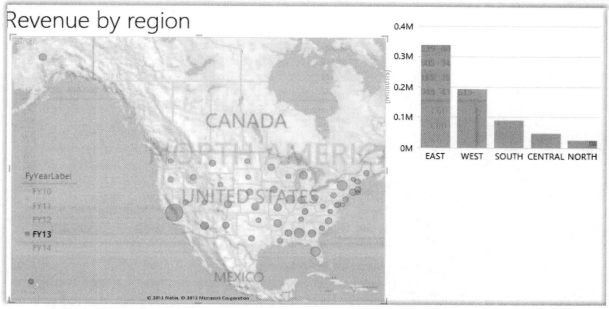

*Figure 5.41: Adding a map to the canvas.*

### Power View Tip: Power View Maps

It's pretty amazing that Power View can show this map without you having to specify anything about the data. Power View asks the Bing maps engine for the location that you want to visualize. Bing knows how to visualize interesting locations, like Safeco field in Seattle and even the PSV soccer stadium in my hometown, Eindhoven.

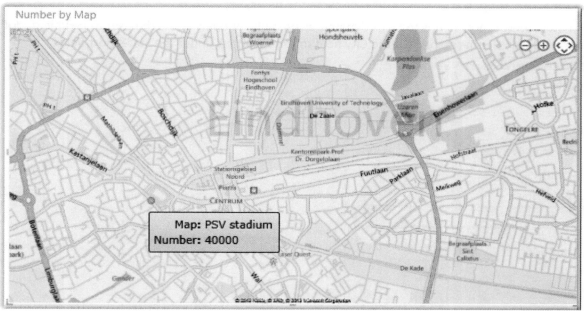

*Figure 5.42: Visualizing data around the world, no latitude or longitude required.*

Of course, there is one drawback to this approach: You need to have an active Internet connection to use maps. Sometimes the data doesn't show up correctly because several cities or towns around the world might have the same name or other issues. This help document covers how to solve such problems: http://ppivot.us/omg7L.

Jim wants to highlight each region in the chart, so he decides to associate a different color with each dot on the chart, based on the group it belongs to. He wants to group the states by region, so he drags a region into the color area of the field well. As a result, Power View adds a legend to the visualization, but Jim doesn't want it and removes it by using the Layout tab. He now has the chart he wants.

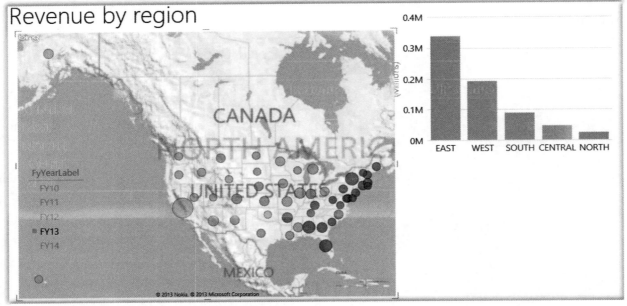

*Figure 5.43: Adding color to a map visualization.*

### Power View Tip: The Power View Field Well

Unlike in Excel, in Power View, the field well (see figure 5.33) changes with each visualization. Certain areas make sense only for certain visualizations. For example, a map chart has a Locations area and a Size area, whereas a line chart has a Values area and an Axis area. Whenever you switch between visualizations, Power View tries to map the fields between areas, if possible; when it's not possible, Power View discards the fields.

This Power View report needs to be as dynamic as possible, and Jim wants the user to be able to drill down to the city level. He therefore adds the City field to the Locations under the StateShort field.

Drag fields between areas below:

TILE BY

Σ SIZE

Sum of Revenue ▼

LOCATIONS

StateShort ▼

City ▼

LONGITUDE          LATITUDE

COLOR

Region ▼

VERTICAL MULTIPLES

HORIZONTAL MULTIPLES

*Figure 5.44: Multiple levels of location navigation.*

Now when the user double-clicks the region in the chart, Power View automatically zooms in to show the cities that belong to that region.

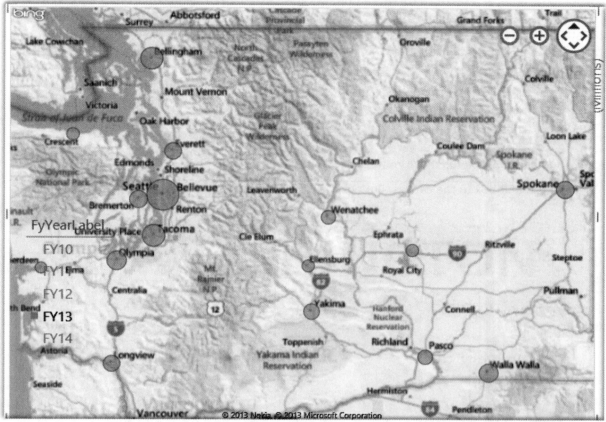

*Figure 5.45: After zooming into the Washington state Region it now show each city with revenue.*

At the top of the map, the up arrow allows the user to navigate back to the region view.

Next, Jim wants to show the number of markets per month for the currently selected fiscal year. Jim selects the Nr of Markets calculated field and adds FyMonthLabel to the field before changing the visualization into a line chart. He again decides to remove the title and to add data labels by using the Power View Layout tab.

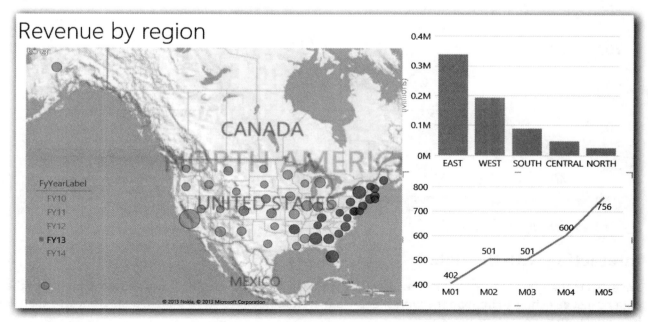

*Figure 5.46: Adding more visualization to the Power View canvas.*

Before Jim continues adding more visualizations, he wants to add his own labels above the charts. To do this, he selects Power View, Text Box.

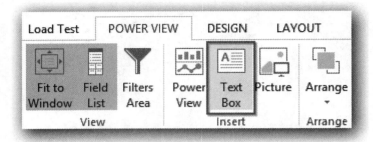

*Figure 5.47: Adding a textbox to Power View.*

Power View adds a text box to the canvas. Jim types VTT by Region in the text box and puts it above the chart.

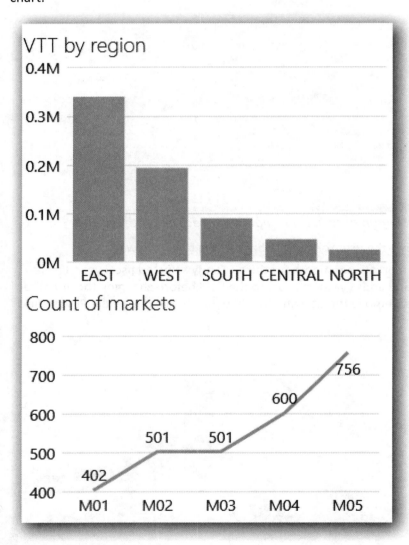

*Figure 5.48: Labeling the charts.*

## Interacting with the Data

Jim expects the users to want to use the interactivity Power View has to offer. It will allow them to filter the data by just selecting an item on the worksheet. He therefore needs to show data in a different way than he would with a more static presentation.

## Power View Tip: Cross-Filtering in Power View

Power View allows users to easily bring data to life. They can cross-filter data by simply clicking a data point in a data visualization on the canvas, and Power View automatically filters all other data visualizations on the same canvas. For example, if you click Minnesota on the following map, Power View automatically cross-filters the two other charts to show only the data for Minnesota.

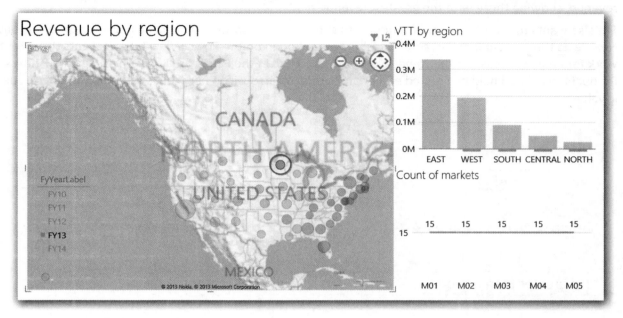

*Figure 5.49: Cross-filtering the charts for a single region.*

In the bar chart, you can immediately see how Minnesota is faring against other regions, which are grayed out but still visible.

Now if you click the East region in the bar chart you see that other regions are grayed out but still visible, so you can still easily make comparisons. The same sort of thing happens with the map: The states in the East region are highlighted, while the rest fade into the background. However, the chart shows just the East region selection and not the previous values.

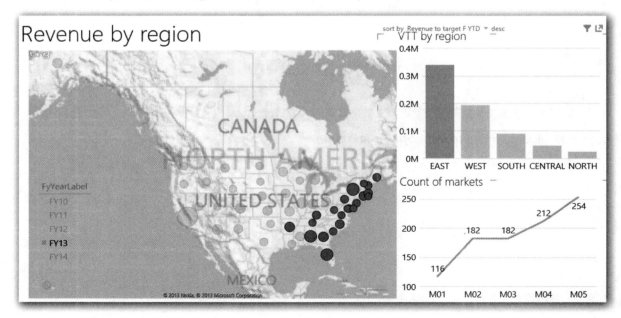

*Figure 5.50: Highlighting the map with the chart selection.*

This is an important feature that users love because it allows them to really play with the data. It is also a very popular feature for those using Power View for presentations. A presenter can answer many questions on the spot by selecting values in the chart or adding filters to the Filters area. There's no need to come back another time with a new report.

Jim wants to be able to see the top products and their revenue. He adds Sum of Revenue and Product-Name to the canvas and changes the visualization from a table to a bar chart. He wants to show the best products first, so he changes the sort to Sum of Revenue, in descending order. This sorts all the products by revenue, showing those with the greatest revenue first.

Jim also wants to reduce the list of products to show only the products that contributed to the most sales. He selects the chart and makes sure the Filters area is open on the Power View tab. He wants this filter to work for only this visualization, so he selects the Chart tab in the Filters area. Here he drags the Pct of All Products calculated field he created earlier and clicks the arrow icon next to it so that he can filter a specific value.

Figure 5.51: Adding filters to a specific visualization.

He selects all products that account for more than 2% to filter the number of products to a more manageable subset. Next, he removes the title and adds data bars.

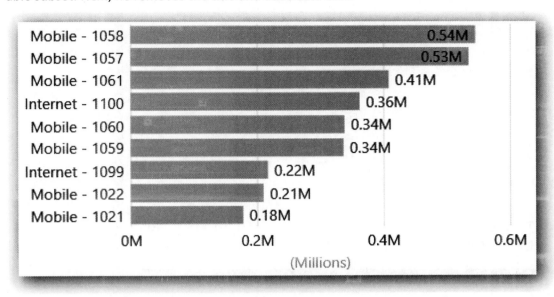

Figure 5.52: Visualizing the top performing products

## Using Multiples to Compare Data

Jim wants to compare revenue over time by region in a visual way. He starts by selecting FyMonthLabel and Sum of Revenue for a new visualization that he makes into a line chart.

### Power View Tip: Using Multiples in Power View

A great feature in Power View called Multiples allows you to compare a series of identical charts. Multiples are small repeating charts that make it easier to compare many different values at the same time. To make comparing these charts easy, Power View automatically synchronizes the horizontal and vertical axes.

Jim wants to compare the revenue for each region, so he drags Region under Vertical Multiples in the field well.

Drag fields between areas below:

TILE BY

*Not available with multiples*

Σ VALUES

Sum of Revenue ▼

AXIS

FyMonthLabel ▼

LEGEND

VERTICAL MULTIPLES

⊕ Region ▼

HORIZONTAL MULTIPLES

Figure 5.53: Vertical multiples in the field well

The chart will now be repeated for each region.

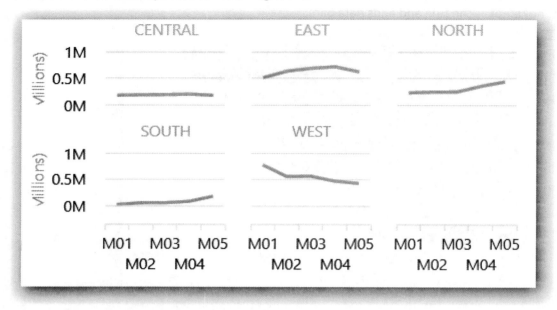

*Figure 5.54: Vertical multiples used in a chart.*

As a finishing touch, Jim adds labels to his charts. His Power View report is now complete.

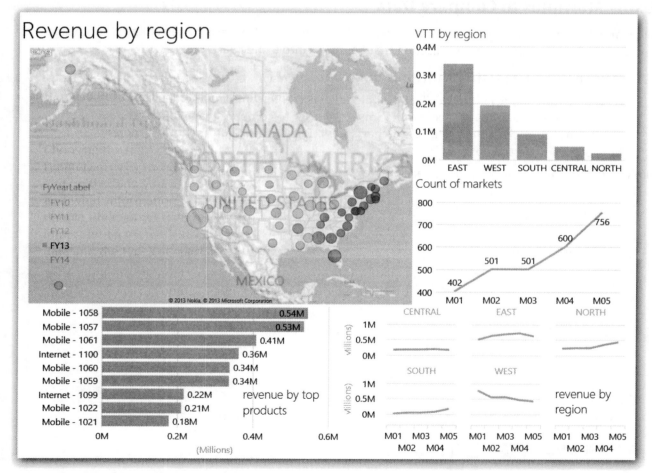

*Figure 5.55: The finished Power View report.*

## Showing a List of Items in Power View

Jim wants to show a detailed report for his products in a new Power View report. To insert a new Power View sheet, he selects the Insert tab then Insert Power View. He then adds to the Power View canvas the product name and several calculated fields, such as Sum of Revenue, Sum of Revenue Target, Target Revenue, Sum of Units, and Sum of Usage. This gives him a rather boring table of metrics, by product name.

Click here to add a title

| ProductName | Sum of Revenue | Sum of RevenueTarget | Revenuetarget | Sum of Units | Sum of Usage |
|---|---|---|---|---|---|
| Business Premium Line | $1,188,410.40 | $1,397,120.51 | 1,397,120.51 | 79,746,850 | 60,102,276.05 |
| Business Unlimited | $391,952.11 | $453,845.16 | 453,845.16 | 21,967,050 | 16,636,706.55 |
| Domestic Unlimited | $165,415.27 | $191,733.11 | 191,733.11 | 9,065,900 | 6,884,916.69 |
| Freedom Calling | $600,705.68 | $700,262.89 | 700,262.89 | 123,625,750 | 93,318,676.70 |
| Freedom Unlimited | $614,479.13 | $709,729.84 | 709,729.84 | 129,405,500 | 98,083,396.47 |
| International Unlimited | $185,243.69 | $216,077.44 | 216,077.44 | 10,265,000 | 7,751,266.12 |
| Internet - 1039 | $267,743.65 | $316,132.21 | 316,132.21 | 26,908,000 | 19,918,349.88 |
| Internet - 1040 | $284,662.68 | $334,908.08 | 334,908.08 | 28,776,000 | 21,431,071.99 |
| Internet - 1041 | $288,225.84 | $337,847.15 | 337,847.15 | 143,925,000 | 107,501,017.20 |
| Internet - 1042 | $286,529.67 | $337,677.94 | 337,677.94 | 143,970,000 | 107,233,901.18 |
| Internet - 1043 | $267,923.28 | $313,103.02 | 313,103.02 | 26,951,000 | 20,053,335.02 |
| Internet - 1044 | $266,069.35 | $311,789.99 | 311,789.99 | 26,812,000 | 19,795,441.48 |
| Internet - 1045 | $270,778.90 | $318,065.89 | 318,065.89 | 135,115,000 | 100,066,998.47 |
| Internet - 1046 | $271,470.43 | $319,298.68 | 319,298.68 | 135,865,000 | 100,749,416.76 |
| Internet - 1050 | $993,119.11 | $1,168,766.06 | 1,168,766.06 | 428,180,000 | 322,842,121.68 |
| Internet - 1080 | $374,031.75 | $458,042.30 | 458,042.30 | 33,645,000 | 25,226,222.66 |

*Figure 5.56: A table of product values.*

Jim decides to change the table into a card view. This view displays the data from each row in the table, laid out in a card format, like an index card.

*Figure 5.57: Card view.*

### Power View Tip: Images in Power View

A great way to add more value to a visualization is to include images. This will make the visualization much friendlier and easier to recognize. For example, you might use images for countries, products, or employees.

When you want to use images in Power View, you probably need to work with your IT department to load images in Power View because getting the images into the right format can be difficult. For more information, see http://ppivot.us/yYnYF.

The card view shows products in a visual and detailed way. In order for this view to really work, it should be possible to filter the results. Jim wants to filter the list to show only the products for the current fiscal year, so he opens up the Filters Area and adds the Current FY Year filter to the Table Filter.

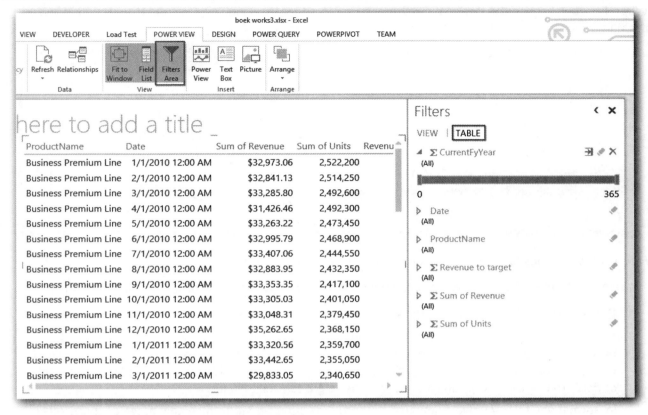

*Figure 5.58: Adding CurrentFyYear to the Table Filter*

Unfortunately, the field doesn't behave as Jim expects. It show the value 365 for the value when he wants it set to 1. He notices that Power View thinks this field is a field to aggregate because it has the sigma sign in front of it; therefore, the setting 365 means that it aggregates every day for the entire year. Jim knows how to discourage Power View from doing this. He opens the Power Pivot windows and selects the CurrentFyYear column and then selects Advanced, Summarize By, Do Not Summarize.

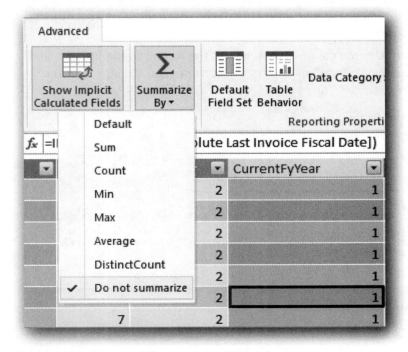

*Figure 5.59: Changing the summary behavior.*

When Jim goes back to the Power View sheet, he notices that the sigma sign is gone from the field list, and the filter now shows 0 and 1 as selections.

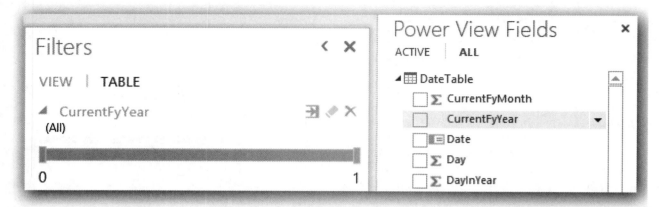

*Figure 5.60: Changes to the summary behavior affecting the field list*

Jim selects 1 to filter the card view to show only the calculated field values for the current fiscal year.

### Power View Tip: Power View's Reporting Properties

Power View is all about creating visualizations quickly and easily from any data set. Users can improve or change the default experience when using a field or table in Power View. For example, they can change the default aggregation a field should use when selected in the field list, what list of fields to use when selecting a table, or how to group certain fields.

In normal day-to-day Power View use, you probably won't need to take advantage of these settings, but in situations like the one Jim encountered, knowing that they exist might save you a few hours.

For an extensive list of reporting properties and their usage, see this help topic: http://ppivot.us/Ufs2W.

Jim wants to show the revenue and revenue target for each month of the current fiscal year. He wants them to appear next to each other. He adds the Sum of Revenue and Sum of RevenueTarget calculations to a new visualization. Next he adds FyYearLabel to the visualization to split the calculations and month, and then he adds the table filter to filter CurrentFyYear only.

Jim changes the visualization from table to clustered column chart, moves the legend to the bottom, and turns off the title. He can now compare the results for all months in the current year and also filter the products in the card view by month.

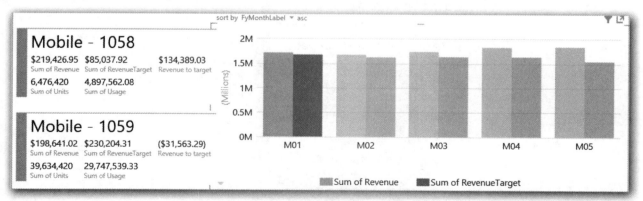

*Figure 5.61: Cross-filtering results by month.*

## Visualizing the Relationship Between Calculations over Time

The last visualization Jim wants to add to his report is something that will allow users to view products and see and compare various numeric values for each value over time. He starts by adding PoductName, Sum of Revenue, and Sum of Units to the canvas. He then changes the visualization to a scatter chart.

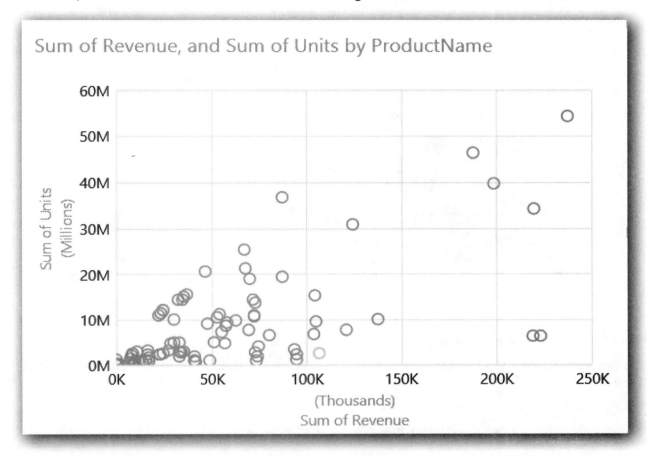

*Figure 5.62: A scatter chart showing products in two dimensions.*

Power View shows a dot for each product by Sum of Revenue on the x-axis and Sum of Units on the y-axis. The product in the upper-right corner is the product that made the most revenue while shipping the most units. Interestingly, units below that one managed to get the same amount of revenue but with fewer units sold. This seems like an interesting grouping for products.

Jim wants to highlight the target revenue for each product. He can turn the scatter chart into a bubble chart by adding a new calculated field to the Size area of the scatter chart. Now this calculated field determines the size of each product bubble. Jim can immediately see that the products he observed earlier actually did really well and made much more revenue than was targeted.

Sum of Revenue, Sum of Units, and Revenue to target by Product

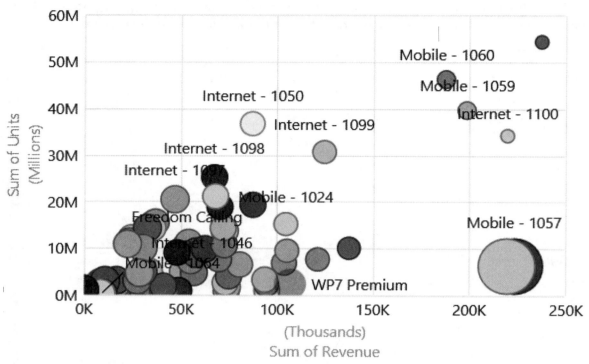

*Figure 5.63: A scatter chart made into a bubble chart.*

Now Jim wants to allow this chart to show the changes over time. He adds Date to the Play Axis area in the field well.

*Figure 5.64: A scatter/bubble chart field provides lots of options.*

Jim can now run the visualization over time and track the changes to products over time.

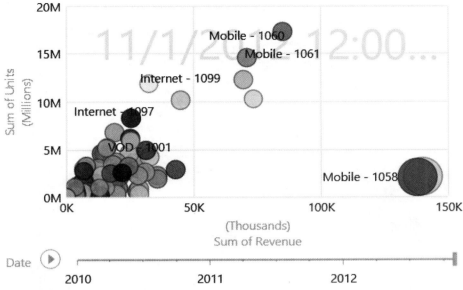

*Figure 5.65: A scatter/bubble chart with a play axis.*

One of the features of the Power View scatter/bubble chart that Jim loves the most is the option to see the changes over time for each bubble on the chart by just selecting one of the bubbles. In this way, he can easily see the changes over time and also cross-filter all other charts on the canvas. Jim now has the interaction he was looking for.

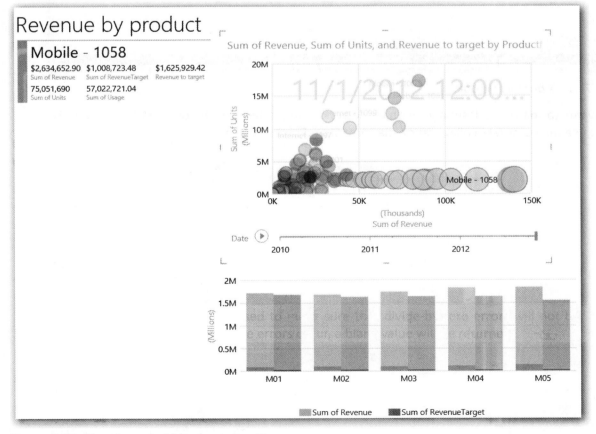

*Figure 5.66: Showing a bubble chart over time.*

Jim removes the title of the chart. He notices that he needs to give both of his Power View worksheets proper names. He names the current one Revenue by Products and the other one Revenue by Regions. Jim now has a dashboard with supporting reports that he is really happy with for a first release.

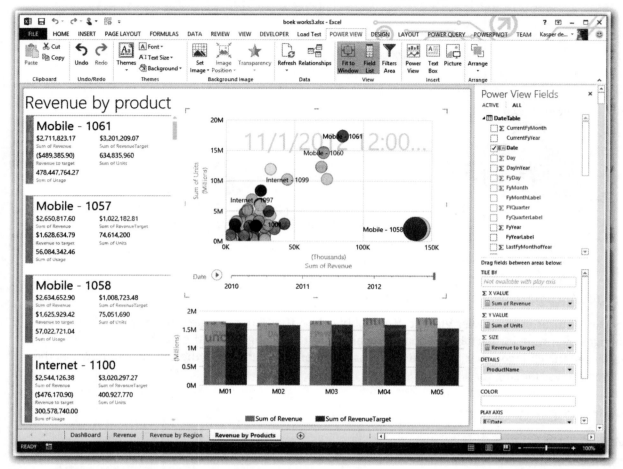

*Figure 5.67: Jim's final workbook.*

Jim now wants to share this dashboard with his coworkers and other stakeholders in the company. He decides to use the corporate collaboration platform SharePoint to do this.

# 6- Sharing Dashboards and Reports Within an Organization

Often the goal of creating a dashboard or a report is to share it with others, to help them gain insights into the information shared. Microsoft gives you a few ways to share a workbook with others:

- **Put it somewhere on the network or send it by email:** This is the traditional way of sharing data with others, but it has some flaws that are especially pronounced when using Power Pivot. Power Pivot can work with large amounts of data, so a file can be quite large. This makes opening it over a network or emailing it difficult. The other downside is that not everyone is able to open a Power Pivot workbook because it requires access to Excel on the local machine. Fortunately, most organizations and individuals have Excel installed. When using Excel 2010, you need to have Power Pivot installed before you can open the file, and not everyone has that. Excel 2013 doesn't have this issue because the Power Pivot engine ships in all versions of Excel. Still, as we noticed in chapter 1, not all versions of Excel 2013 allow you to consume a Power Pivot report.

- **Share it to SharePoint:** Many large organizations have Microsoft SharePoint installed. SharePoint is Microsoft's collaboration platform, which gives you a secure place to store, organize, share, and access information from almost any device. All you need is a web browser. When SharePoint is set up correctly, it can also handle PowerPivot workbooks, which means you can share a workbook to Share-Point once and let others consume its reports by using a web browser. They don't need to download the workbook or have Excel installed on their machines. Another benefit is that the author can auto-matically refresh the data in the workbook without having to even open the workbook in Excel.

Two great resources on Power Pivot for SharePoint are the books *Professional Microsoft Power-Pivot for Excel and SharePoint by Harinath, Pihlgren and Lee* (see http://ppivot.us/FAVnb) and *Warren, Teixeira Neto, Misner, Sanders, Helmers by Business Intelligence in Microsoft SharePoint 2013* (see http://ppivot.us/fvEv5).

- **Share it to Office 365 and Power BI:** Office 365 and Power BI offer the full power of SharePoint without requiring the resources needed to install and maintain SharePoint on a local machine or net-work. Power BI provides a new and exciting way to visualize data, share discoveries, and collaborate in intuitive new ways. Microsoft provides the Power BI service and ensures that the functionality you need is up and running when you need it. Microsoft continuously adds functionality to the service, without requiring the user to update software locally.

The next two sections discuss sharing a workbook using SharePoint and Office 365 with Power BI. Most often you will have access to one or the other.

## Sharing to SharePoint 2010/2013

Jim has finished his report and is ready to share it with his coworkers and managers. He opens his web browser and navigates to the Contoso finance team's site on SharePoint, which is set up to use the Power Pivot gallery.

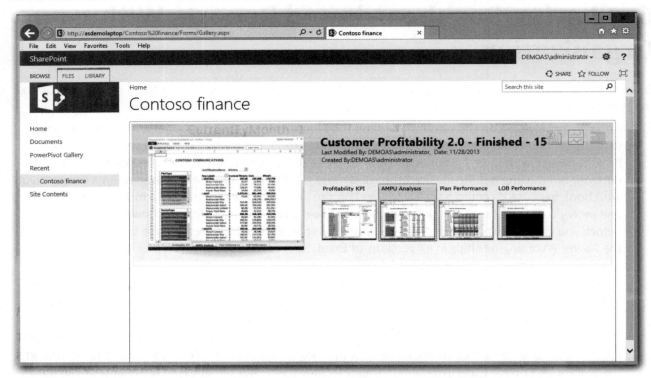

*Figure 6.1: The Contoso finance team site, which uses the Power Pivot gallery on SharePoint.*

### SharePoint Tip: Power Pivot Gallery

The Power Pivot gallery allows users to see workbooks that contain Power Pivot models in a special way. The Power Pivot gallery is available only when SharePoint has been set up to work with Power Pivot workbooks. For more information, see this help topic: http://ppivot.us/hnmlJ.

The site already has a workbook that Jim used previously to calculate the customer profitability for Contoso. Jim now adds the new DashBoard workbook to the SharePoint site and selects Files, Upload Document.

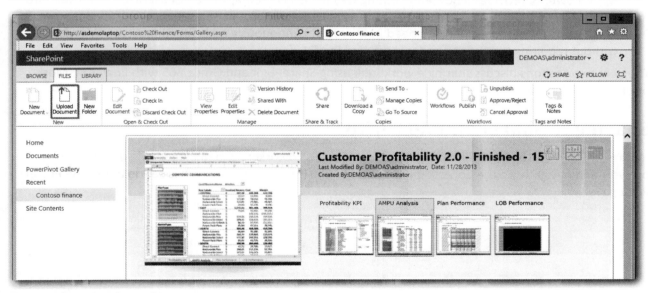

*Figure 6.2: Uploading a file.*

Next, Jim selects the workbook on his machine to upload the workbook to the site. The workbook is initially in a temporary state, indicated by the thumbnails.

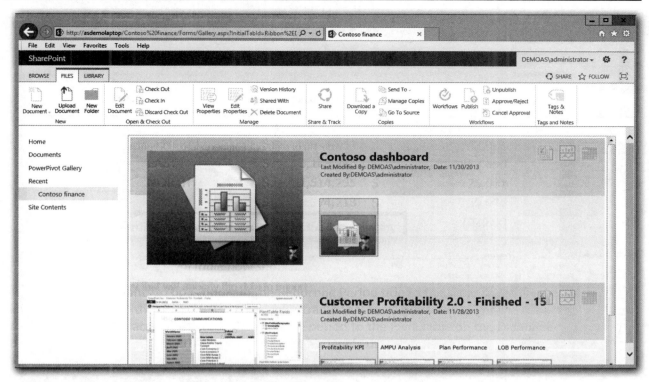

*Figure 6.3: The new file added to the site, without thumbnails.*

After a minute or so, the thumbnails start to show up indicating that the workbook has completed loading and processing.

> These thumbnails are based on the worksheets in the uploaded workbook, showing screenshots of the real data on the spreadsheets.

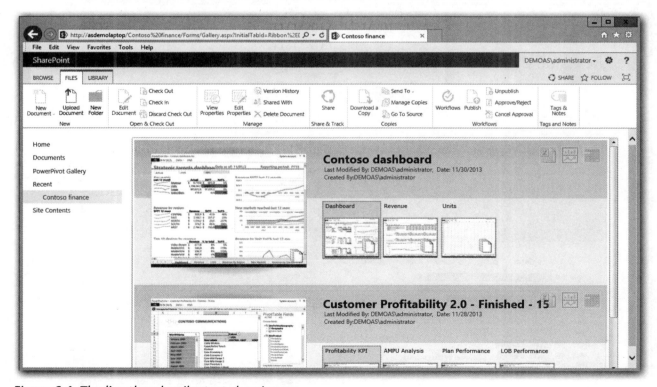

*Figure 6.4: The live thumbnails start showing up.*

Jim clicks a thumbnail to open the workbook in the web browser.

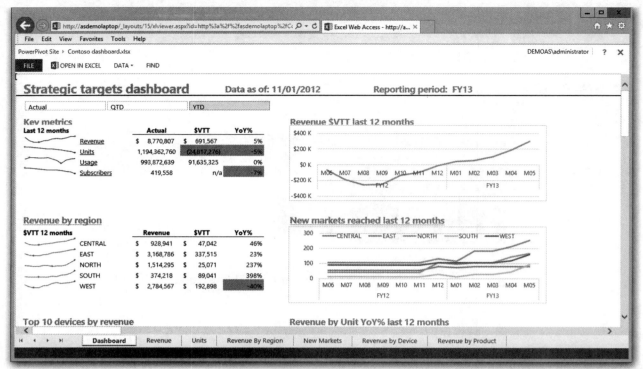

*Figure 6.5: Opening the workbook in the browser.*

In the browser, Jim is able to use the same slicers and interactivity that he is used to when using Excel on his desktop machine. He can switch between worksheets without a problem, and his Power View worksheet shows up in the web browser for browsing.

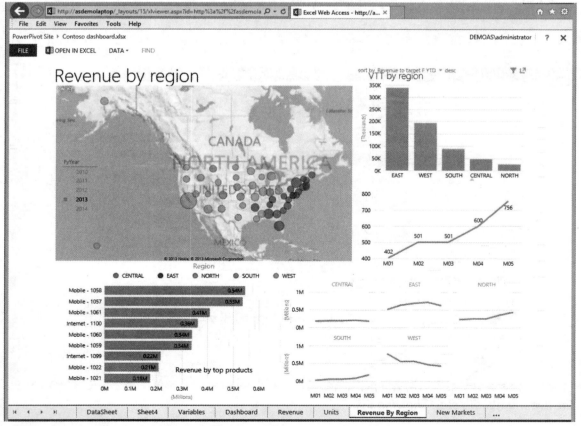

*Figure 6.6: The Power View report in the web browser.*

Anyone who has access to this workbook can view and interact with the reports by using a browser, even without having Excel installed on the machine.

Before giving his users access to the workbook, Jim wants to make sure everyone sees the most recent data. He wants this workbook to have fresh data every week. Sharing the workbook to SharePoint allows him to schedule a refresh of the data without downloading and updating the workbook on his desktop.

Jim goes back to the site and clicks the Manage Data Refresh icon for his dashboard.

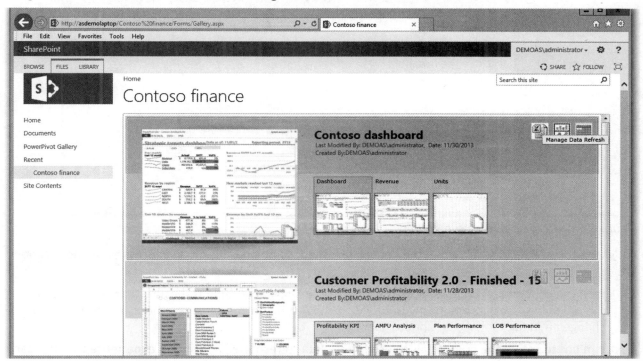

*Figure 6.7: Managing data refreshing.*

In the Manage Data Refresh page that opens up, Jim selects the Data Refresh check box. This enables him to select a schedule. Jim wants his workbook to be refreshed once a week on Sunday, so the data from last week will be added to the workbook the following Monday. To make sure it works, he checks the Also Refresh as Soon as Possible check box to run the refresh immediately.

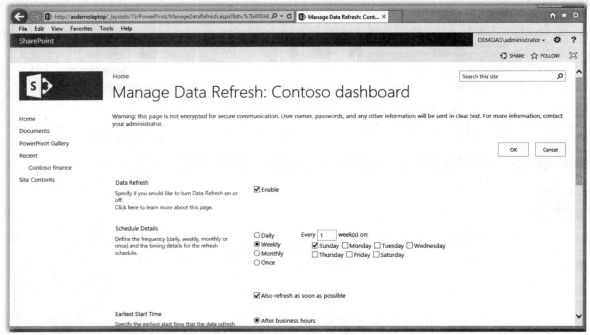

*Figure 6.8: Setting up a refresh schedule.*

Jim wants to receive an email when the data is refreshed, so he adds his email address to the notification list.

> Remember that Jim added special columns in the DateTable table to ensure that the filters on the dashboard are automatically updated to show the current dates—without requiring Jim to change anything to make an update happen.

Next, Jim has to set up the credentials to use for his data refresh. He knows from experience that this can be quite tricky. Jim imported the data into Power Pivot from an Access file on his network. Jim needs to enter his own credentials in order to have the workbook on SharePoint connect to his Access file on the network.

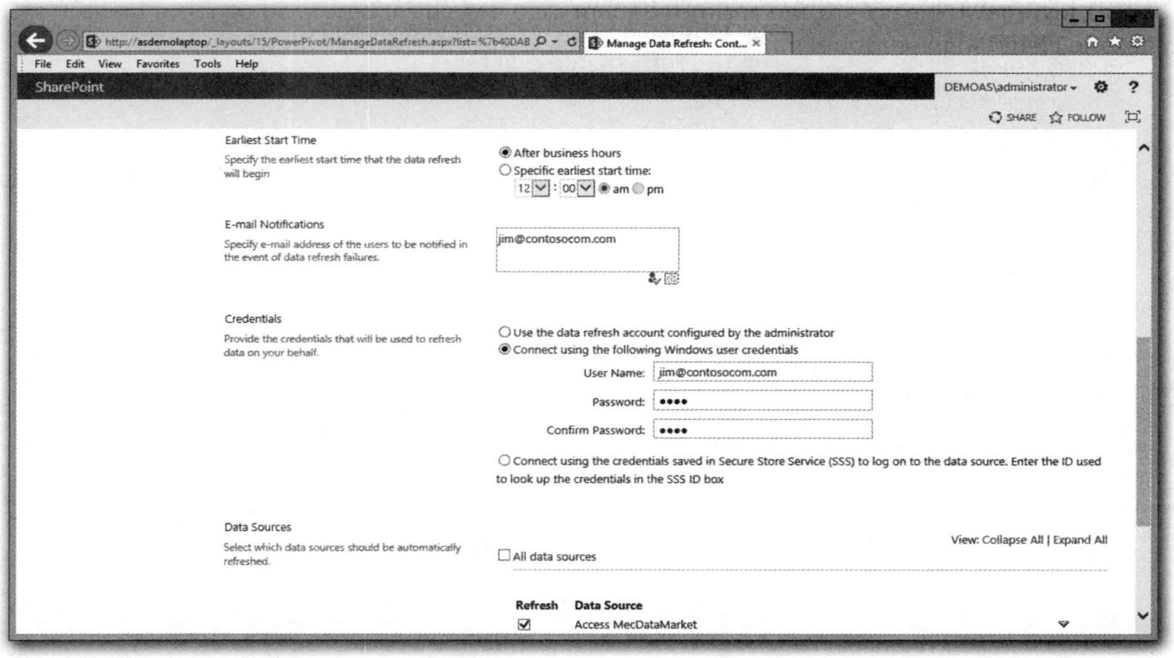

*Figure 6.9: Adding notifications and security.*

## SharePoint Tip: Refreshing Data from SharePoint

When refreshing data from SharePoint, make sure the SharePoint machine can access the data in your Power Pivot workbook. Usually this isn't a problem with a database, but when you use files (such as CSV or Access files), it can cause issues. When you use files, move them to a network share or find a secure place in the cloud. These places can often be reached from anywhere. For more detailed information, see this help article: http://ppivot.us/flDqa.

Keep in mind that when you use Excel 2013 and Power View reports, the data refresh doesn't work. You have to remove the Power View worksheets from the workbook in order for refresh to work. For more information, see this help topic: http://ppivot.us/PnH5n.

Jim wants to refresh the entire workbook so he doesn't need to change the Data Sources setting. Jim finally clicks OK to apply the schedule.

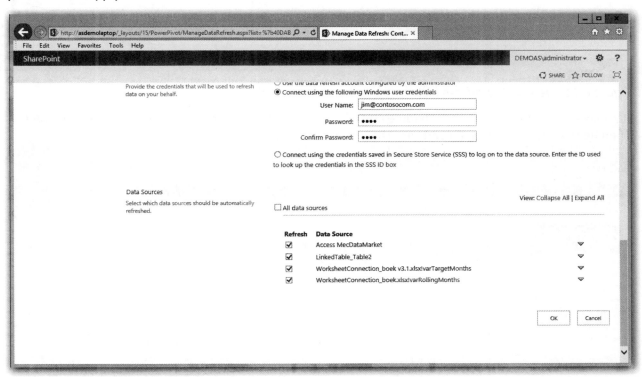

*Figure 6.10: Applying the schedule.*

After Jim applies the schedule, the refresh runs for the first time. To see if the refresh is successful, Jim clicks the Manage Data Refresh icon on the SharePoint site. On the refresh page history, Jim sees that the refresh has failed.

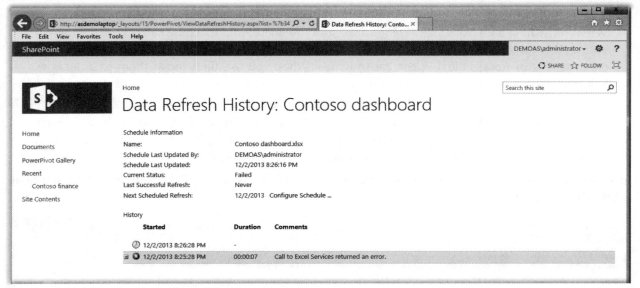

*Figure 6.11: Viewing the refresh history.*

Jim makes some updates to the schedule and ensures that the SharePoint site can reach the document. Then he tries the refresh again and sees that this one is successful.

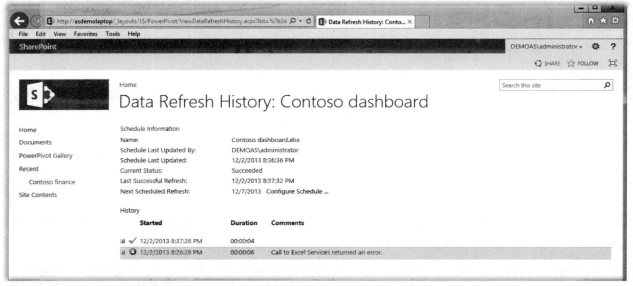

*Figure 6.12: A successful refresh.*

### SharePoint Tip: Handling Refresh Problems

Sometimes it can be hard to figure out why a refresh isn't working. The error messages you see in the history aren't always very insightful. When you open a workbook in the Excel web application and click Refresh, Excel tries to refresh the data in the workbook from the source. If an error occurs during the refresh, you can find more details here on the refreshing issue than at the data refresh history page.

For more information on troubleshooting problems with refreshing, see this blog post by Denny Lee: http://ppivot.us/f22cH.

Now that the workbook is refreshing, Jim wants to share it with his manager and coworkers. He selects the document and then selects Files, Share.

*Figure 6.13: Sharing a workbook with others.*

In the Share 'Contoso dashboard' window that appears, Jim selects his team and then clicks Can Edit. This allows those team members to make changes and update the refresh schedule. For others who need to consume this workbook, Jim selects Can View to allow them consume the workbook but not make any changes.

*Figure 6.14: Determining the user names to share the workbook with*

### SharePoint Tip: Securing Your Workbooks

In SharePoint, a workbook is available only to those who have access to the site or workbook. Someone who doesn't have access to a file won't be able to find or see the file in SharePoint. He or she won't even see the thumbnail.

If you want to see who has access to a file, select the workbook, go to the file, and click Shared With. You then see a list of users who have access to the workbook. It's a good idea to test the access level users have by testing. It's better to be safe than sorry!

Users whom Jim has allowed to access his workbook can also use the Power Pivot model in the workbook as a data source for new reports. His users can connect to the workbook as if it were a separate data source by using the Open New Excel Workbook and Create New Power View Report icons from a workbook in the Power Pivot Gallery.

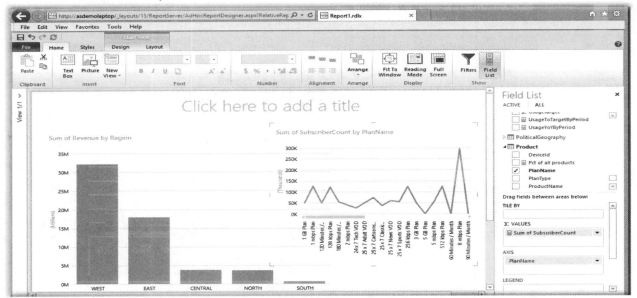

*Figure 6.15: A new Power View report using Power Pivot for Excel workbook as source.*

# Sharing to Office 365 and Power BI

Contoso Communications is thinking about moving its collaboration platform to Microsoft Office 365. Management thinks that using SharePoint in the cloud will save resources and money because Contoso won't have to maintain its own servers and do its own maintenance and patching.

Jim is using his dashboard and reports as a pilot project for Contoso to try out Office 365 and Power BI. He signs up for a preview of the service at http://ppivot.us/5q1Yq.

After Jim creates an account, he logs in to Office 365, which automatically opens in the SharePoint Online site. He uploads a test workbook to the site to test whether it works—and he find that it does.

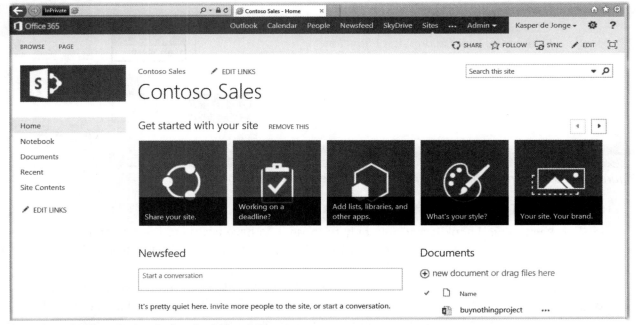

*Figure 6.16: SharePoint Online in Office 365.*

Jim can upload more workbooks and share them with his colleagues. However, the SharePoint Online site doesn't enable the BI-specific features of Power BI by default.

### Power BI Tip: Getting to Know Power BI

Microsoft Power BI provides a new and exciting way of working with data in a familiar way. Power BI is an add-on to Office 365. When enabled, it offers a set of BI capabilities inside Excel and SharePoint online.

Power BI offers a cohesive set of tools inside Excel for working with data in a number of ways:

• **Data discovery and access:** One of the gems of Power BI is Power Query, which allows users to discover relevant data using its search capabilities for data inside and outside the organization. It allows users to access data from a lot of different data sources, including some that were previously not possible from Excel, like Hadoop and HDFS. It also improves import experiences for the already supported data sources like text files, Access and Microsoft SQL Server. Power Query allows you to combine and shape data from multiple, disparate data sources. It provides some great table-shaping features, including merging and appending separate tables, filtering data, splitting columns using delimiters and characters, and unpivoting data. You can use the shaped data in Excel tables or in the Excel data model.

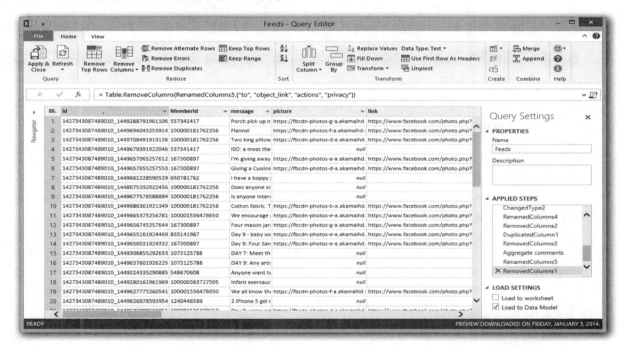

*Figure 6.17: Shaping data in Power Query.*

• **Data modeling:** Power BI allows you do data modeling in Power Pivot, after the data gets imported by Power Query you can optimize it for doing the visualization. For example you can create relationship between tables so you can easily join data from two tables in a Pivot Table, Pivot Chart or Power View. Creating this model is covered throughout this book.

• **Data visualization:** Power BI allows you to do data visualization through Power View for Excel (refer to Chapter 5). Power BI also offer a great Excel 3D visualization add-in, called Power Map, for mapping, exploring, and interacting with geographic data.

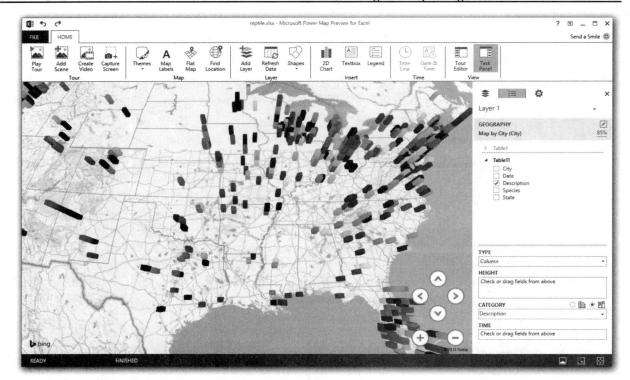

*Figure 6.18: Visualizing data with Power Map.*

Microsoft Power BI also provides a business intelligence infrastructure, bringing together Excel workbook sharing, online collaboration, and IT infrastructure into Office 365.

With SharePoint online, Power BI allows you to create BI sites, which means you can transform any SharePoint online site into a more robust, dynamic location to share and find Excel workbooks, with a visual, interactive view tailored to BI. Power BI sites also provide easy access to other BI features available in Power BI for Office 365. For more on BI sites, see http://ppivot.us/arcxm.

At this writing, the Power BI service is available only as a public preview. When Microsoft officially releases it as a service, Microsoft will take care of most of the heavy lifting for its customers: It will make sure the Power BI service is up and running when you need it, guarantee its performance, and continuously add new functionality without requiring the user to update the software locally. By the time you read this chapter, Microsoft will have released Power BI as a paid service and that may mean that parts of this chapter are outdated or describe processes that work a little differently than presented here.

## Enabling Power BI

After Jim logs in to Office 365, he needs to enable Power BI on his Office 365 SharePoint Online site. Because he signed up for the Power BI preview, he knows it's available for him. Jim clicks Site Contents.

*Figure 6.19: Changing site settings by selecting Site Contents.*

Then Jim wants to add the Power BI application, so he clicks Add an App.

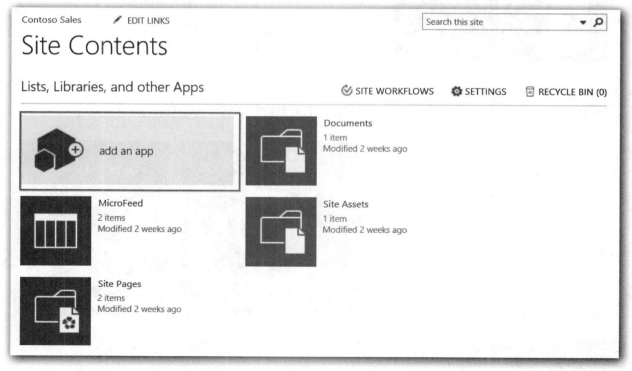

*Figure 6.20: Adding an app to the site.*

Next, Jim selects the Power BI app to add it to the site.

*Figure 6.21: Selecting Power BI.*

Jim selects to trust the app and adds it to the site. The setup process takes a little time. When it is complete, Jim goes back to the site and sees Power BI in the menu.

*Figure 6.22: Power BI is enabled.*

Clicking Power BI takes Jim to a welcome page, where he clicks Use My Own Data to add his own work-books to Power BI.

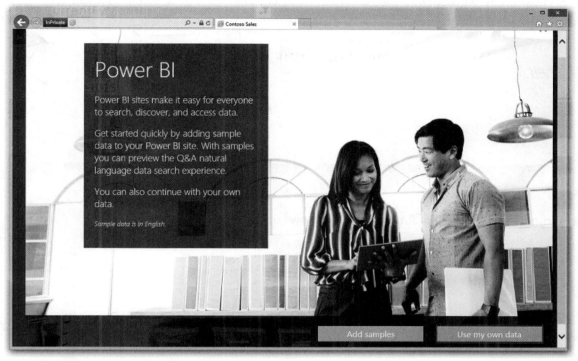

*Figure 6.23: The Power BI welcome page.*

### Power BI Tip: The Power BI Site

The Power BI site transforms your SharePoint site into a site that is more optimized for BI than a regular SharePoint site. It shows documents with a visual, interactive view tailored to BI. The Power BI site also provides easy access to other BI features available in Power BI for Office 365. It's important to understand that all the documents in all the SharePoint document libraries in the site are duplicated in the BI site, which gives the user a different view of the workbooks as well as access to specific BI features such as data refreshing.

Jim now sees the Power BI site.

*Figure 6.24: The Power BI site's main page.*

# Uploading and Enabling a Workbook

Jim uploads his DashBoard workbook to the Power BI site by clicking Add and selecting Upload File.

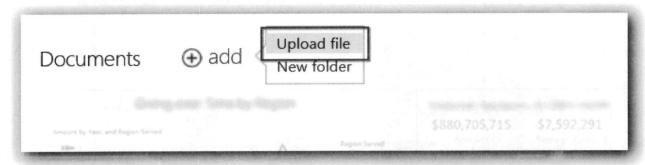

*Figure 6.25: Uploading a file.*

After a few moments, a thumbnail of Jim's workbook shows up on the Power BI site.

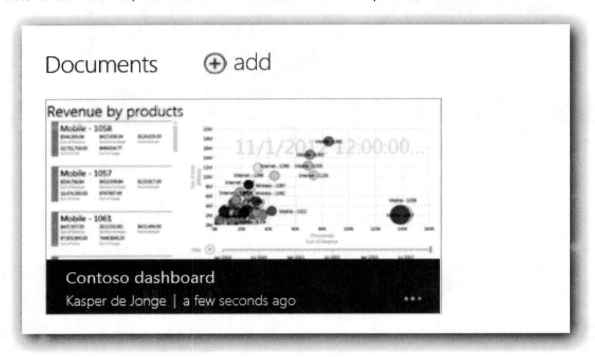

*Figure 6.26: A workbook preview.*

Jim clicks the thumbnail to open the report in Power BI. It looks exactly the same as it does in the on-premise SharePoint software.

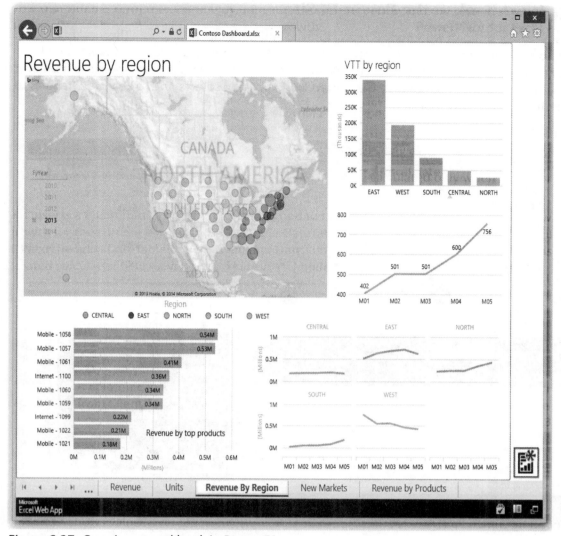

*Figure 6.27: Opening a workbook in Power BI.*

Now, Jim's colleagues who don't have the latest version of Excel 2013 but do have an Office 365 subscription with a Power BI license will be able to use the site and consume his reports without having to install Excel.

### Power BI Tip: Power View HTML 5 Preview

Clicking the icon at the bottom right of the window shown in Figure 6.27 loads any Power View sheet in HTML 5 instead of Silverlight. This allows a more fluid and interactive experience across multiple platforms and devices. At this writing, this is a preview feature, but at some point, the HTML 5 version of Power View will replace the Silverlight version completely.

## Featuring a Workbook at the Power BI Site

Jim has made sure his DashBoard workbook is ready for use, and he wants to promote the workbook so it is very visible to everyone who visits the Power BI site. To do this, Jim needs to feature his workbook so that it displays at the top of the Power BI site. (The Power BI site can feature three workbooks at a time.) Jim clicks the ellipsis (…) next to the Contoso DashBoard workbook and selects Add to Featured Reports to feature the workbook at the Power BI site.

*Figure 6.28: Featuring a workbook.*

The Power BI site now shows the DashBoard workbook right at the top of the page.

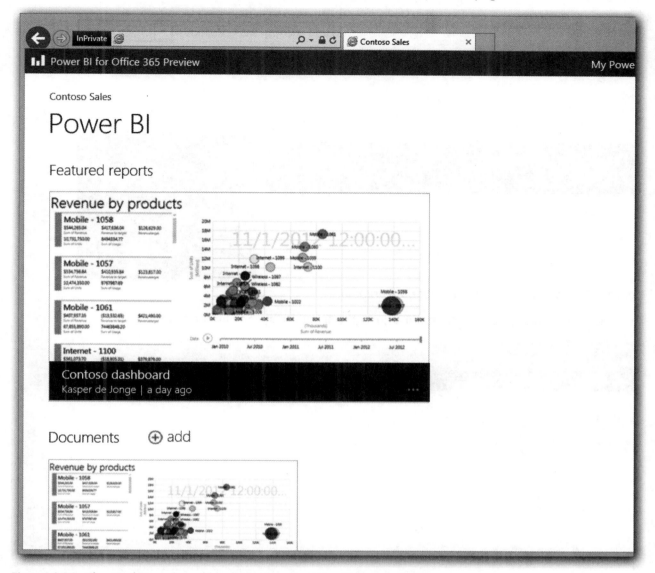

*Figure 6.29: The DashBoard workbook, featured on the BI Power site.*

## Refreshing Data

Jim wants to make sure he can keep the data in his dashboard up to date, even when his workbooks are uploaded to Office 365. He therefore clicks the ellipsis (...) next to the Contoso DashBoard workbook again and selects Schedule Data Refresh.

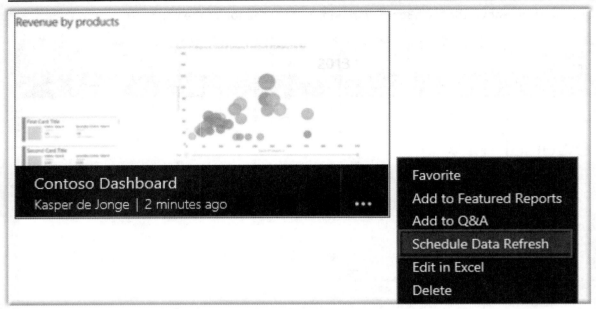

Figure 6.30: Scheduling data refresh for a workbook.

The scheduling page appears, where Jim adjusts the schedule by moving the slider.

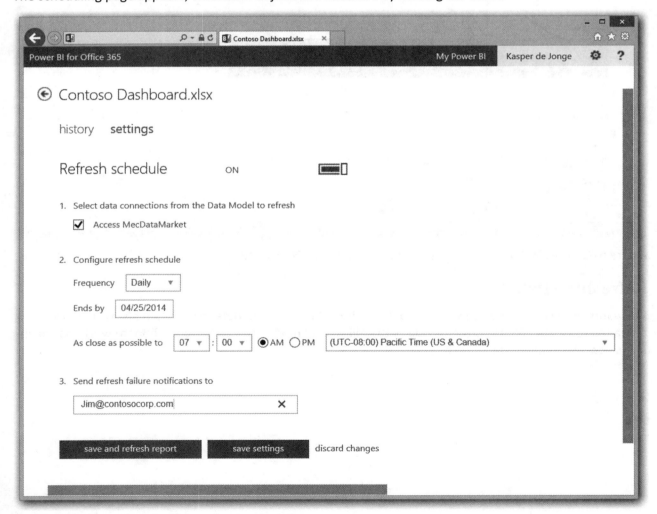

Figure 6.31: Changing the data refresh schedule.

Jim can now set to the data refresh schedule. In this case, he leaves the settings as they are and clicks Save and Refresh Report. The data will now refresh every day, as close to 7 a.m. Pacific time as possible.

### Power BI Tip: How Does Data Refresh Work?

In order for data refresh to work, you (or your IT department) need to set up a data source. For that data source to load data from Office 365 to your local network a gateway needs to be installed on a machine inside the local network.

Now when Power BI refreshes data, it looks for any data sources that are registered and uses a matching algorithm to match the data sources in your workbook with data sources registered on the portal. When it finds an appropriate data source, it uses that connection to refresh the data using the gateway installed on your local network.

In order for Power BI to refresh the workbook data from the Access file on Jim's machine, he needs to set up a data source and gateway. To do this, Jim selects My Power BI, Power BI Admin Center.

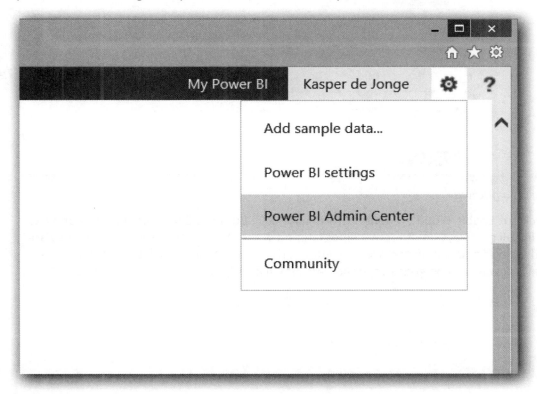

*Figure 6.32: Opening the Power BI Admin Center page.*

In order for Jim to load data from his local machine, he needs to set up a gateway, so he clicks Gateway on the left side of the Power BI Admin Center page.

Power BI admin center

| | gateways | | |
|---|---|---|---|
| system health | | | |
| data sources | ⊕ new gateway | | Search gateways 🔍 |
| gateways | | | |
| role management | **NAME** | **STATUS** | **DESCRIPTION** |
| settings | Gateways deployed: 0 | | |
| get started | | | |

*Figure 6.33: Adding a new gateway.*

On the right side of the page, Jim now sees a list of the gateways installed for Contoso. In this case, of course, there are currently none, so Jim clicks New Gateway to set up a gateway on his work computer. The New Gateway page appears, and Jim adds details for his gateway, including the gateway name.

new gateway

details

install & register

### details

A gateway is used to connect to a data source in your corporate environment. You must have at least one gateway installed in your corporate environment before creating a data source. Learn more

* Name:

ContosoDashboard

Description:

Describe the gateway here

☑ Enable cloud credential store to achieve business continuity for the gateway. ⓘ Learn more

create    cancel

*Figure 6.34: Setting up a gateway.*

Jim selects the check box Enable Cloud Credential Store to Achieve Business Continuity for the Gateway. This means he can install gateways on other machines later on without losing the credentials as they are securely stored in the cloud and can be accessed only through one of the installed gateways. Jim clicks Create to create the gateway, and he gets a page that lets him install the gateway on his computer.

new gateway

details

install & register

### install & register

Download the gateway and then install it on your machine.

download

### register

Copy the key below. Use it to register the gateway installed in your corporate environment. Learn more

Gateway Key:

46aceaee-d678-43bf-a3ea-aa0f5ab117bf@3f6ca58f-181c-4389-a0bd-260ad15b16c4@3f6ca58f-181c-4389-a0bd-260ad15b16c4@West Us#kqvVVCmSrb4Piez8IrJjGnAzgi2t4oyjLCg5BlZsNXl=

finish

*Figure 6.35: Install and register the gateway.*

On the same page Jim selects the key in the Gateway Key box and copies it by pressing Ctrl+C. Then he clicks Download which opens a new window where he can download the gateway. Jim downloads the gateway to his local machine and closes the window.

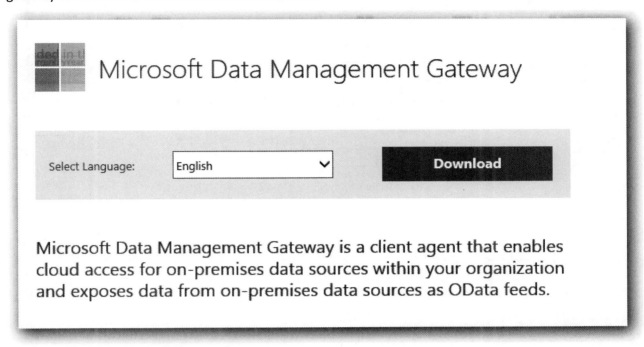

*Figure 6.36: Downloading the gateway*

On the gateway installation page he chooses finish. That will finish his gateway registration and the New Gateway page appears again, this time showing the new gateway added but still needing to be registered.

*Figure 6.37: A gateway has been added and needs to be registered.*

After the Gateway tool is downloaded Jim installs it on his local computer that will host the gateway. When the installation is complete, the tool starts running. Before Jim can do anything else, he needs to register his gateway by pasting in the Gateway key he copied earlier (Ctrl+V) and clicking Register.

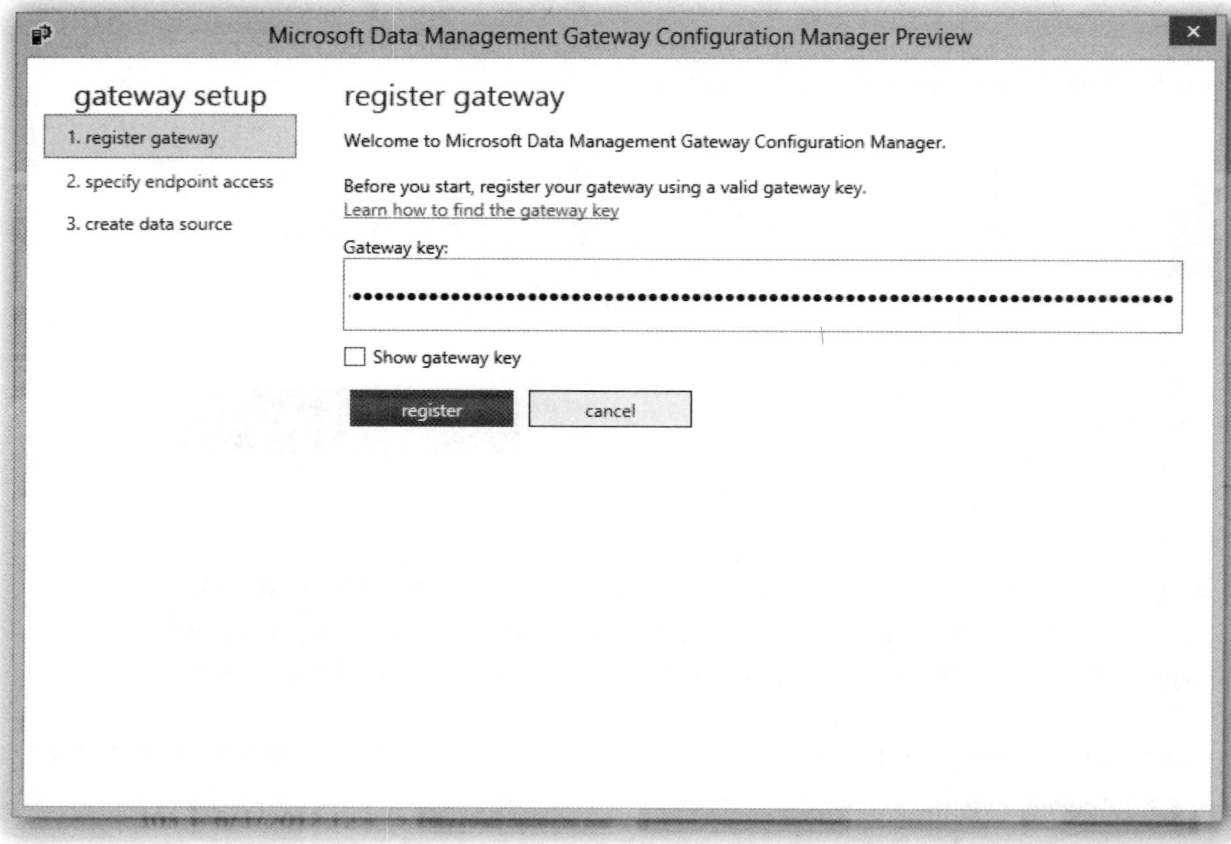

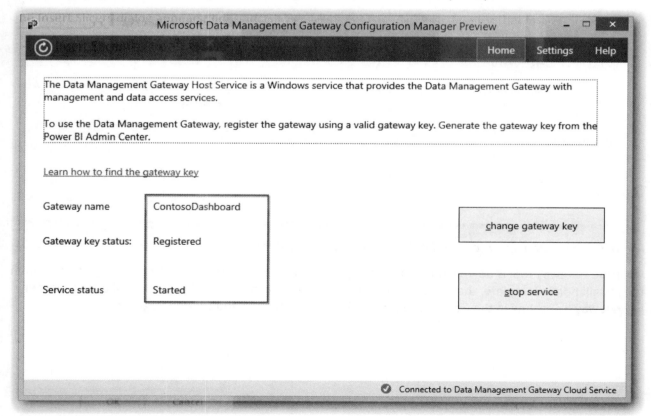

*Figure 6.38: Configuring the gateway tool.*

On the next page he selects HTTP, and clicks Register to finish the Gateway setup.

*Figure 6.39: The configured management tool.*

Jim now goes back to the New Gateway page, where he sees that the gateway is now configured.

*Figure 6.40: The configured gateway.*

Now Jim wants to create a data source, so he goes to the Power BI Admin Center page and clicks Data Sources on the left. He then sees a list of all the data sources (currently empty) on the right.

*Figure 6.41: The data sources list.*

Jim clicks New Data Source so he can configure his new data source.

*Figure 6.42: Creating a new data source.*

He keeps the settings as they are and clicks Next. The Connection Info tab appears, and Jim enters the information needed to connect to his data source.

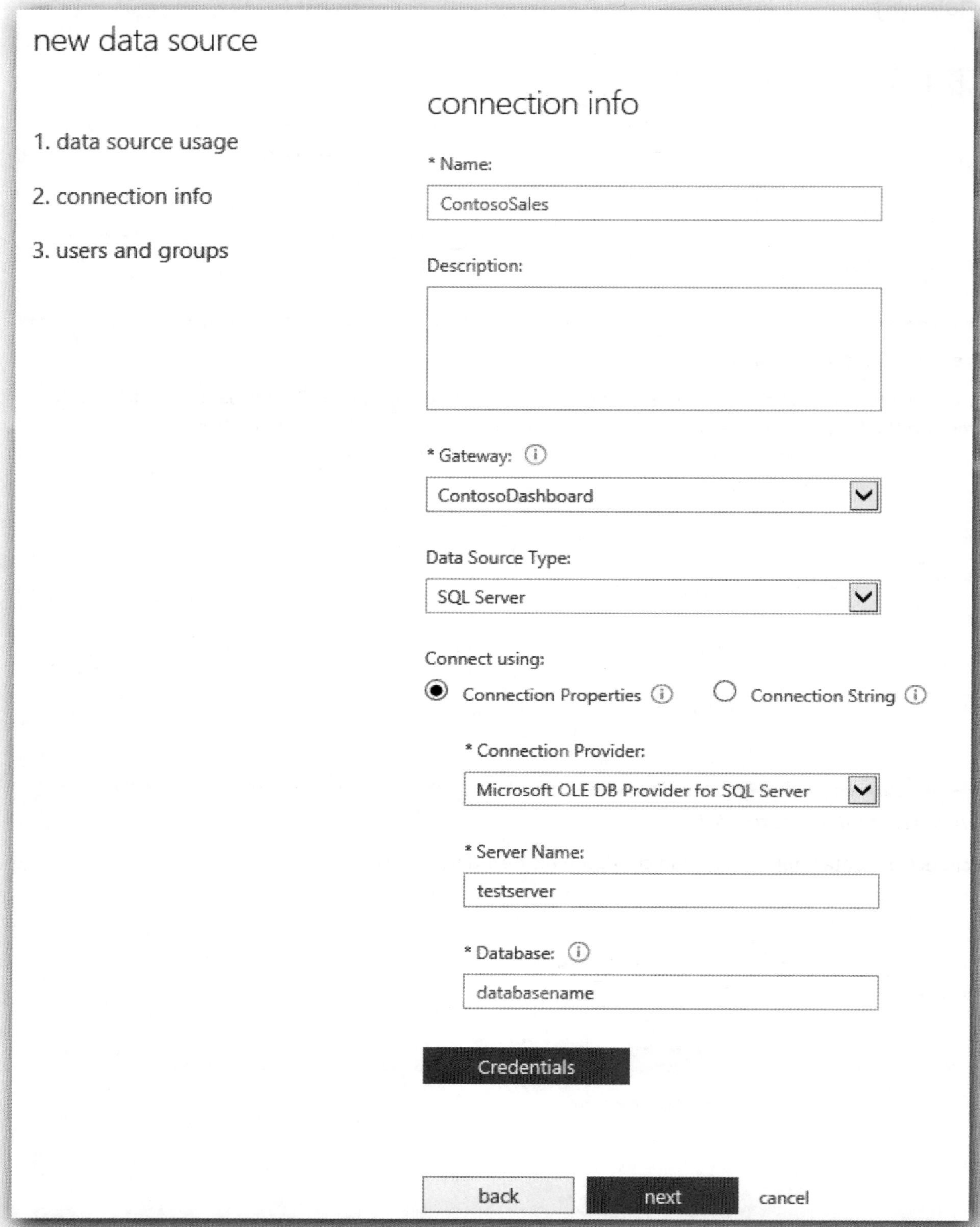

*Figure 6.43: Adding data source connection info.*

## Power BI Tip: On Premise Data Refresh Sources

Initially, Power BI's refresh from on premises data will support will support a limited set of data sources: SQL Server, Oracle, and Windows Azure. More sources will be added to the service in a later update. The scenario of refreshing an Access file as shown in Figure 6.42 doesn't work at this writing but is expected to work soon.

For the latest info on data sources, see this help topic: http://ppivot.us/3Y1qw.

Next, Jim clicks Credentials in Figure 6.43 to open a special app on his computer. This app will store the credentials he adds to this data source on the gateway and not in Office 365. When he's done entering the credentials, Jim clicks OK.

*Figure 6.44: Adding credentials to an app on the local machine.*

Jim clicks Users and Groups on the left side of the New Data Source page so that he can specify which users and groups can use this data source. Jim adds Everyone, meaning all the users that can log into the Power BI site.

*Figure 6.45: Adding users and groups that can use this data source.*

The DashBoard workbook on Office 365 will now have its source data periodically refreshed from the database on Jim's local machine.

## Excel Workbooks on a Mobile Device

Contoso management is excited about Power BI because it allows users to use an app in Windows 8 to interact with workbooks created in Excel. Jim decides to test this app with some of the sample workbooks provided. First he installs the Power BI app from the Windows Store.

*Figure 6.46 The Power BI Windows 8 app.*

A user who opens this app can browse any workbooks that are uploaded to Power BI. By default, the Power BI app has loaded the samples that come with the app.

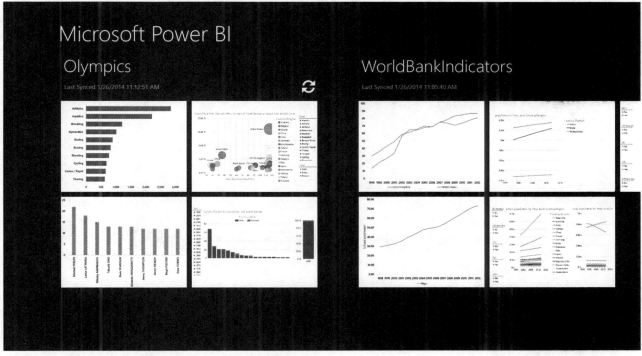

*Figure 6.47: Workbooks loaded into the Power BI app.*

### Power BI Tip: Making a Workbook a Favorite

You can favorite a workbook by selecting the ellipse (...) next to the workbook at the Power BI site and selecting Favorite.

*Figure 6.48: Making a workbook a favorite.*

Now you will be able to find all your favorite workbooks under My Power BI:

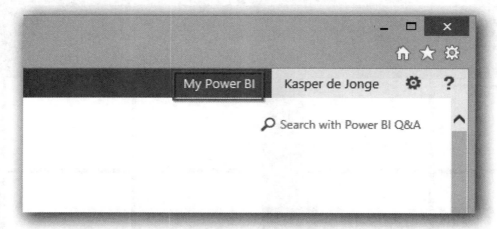

*Figure 6.49: My Power BI.*

In My Power BI you can find a list of all your favorite workbooks:

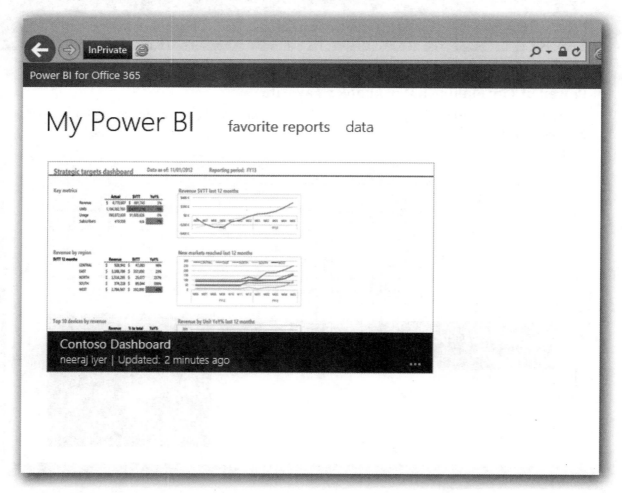

*Figure 6.50: Your favorite workbooks.*

Selecting a workbook in the Power BI app opens a full-fledged report that you can consume as a Windows 8 Modern Application, just as if the app were written to run on your machine by an application developer—but in this case, the report is built in Excel!

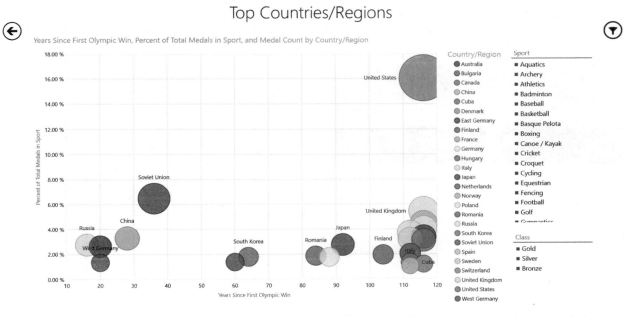

Figure 6.51: Viewing a report in the app.

## Enabling a Workbook for Q&A

Jim has read that Power BI has a Q&A feature that allows users to use natural-language queries to find answers in their own data. This feature makes it possible to start with a question and then refine or expand it. Enabling Q&A on any workbook is pretty straightforward: Simply select the ellipse (…) next to the workbook at the Power BI site and then select Add to Q&A.

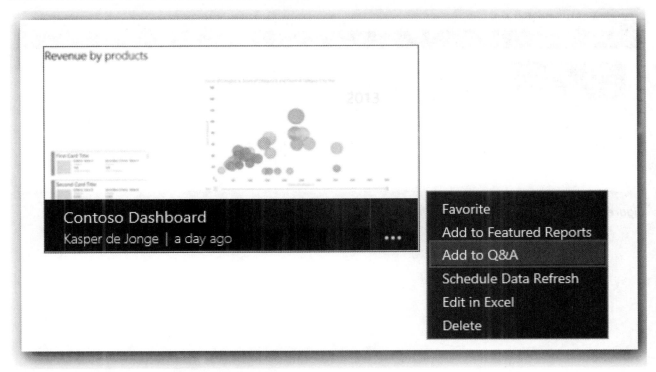

Figure 6.52: Enabling a workbook for Q&A.

Now, all the users of the Power BI site can use Q&A search to explore the DashBoard workbook that Jim created. To try this out on his workbook, Jim clicks Search with Power BI Q&A at the top right of the Power BI site.

*Figure 6.53: Searching with Power BI Q&A.*

Jim can now type a question in the Q&A search page.

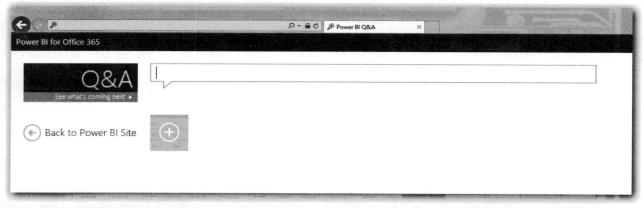

*Figure 6.54: The Power BI Q&A search page.*

As Jim types a question in the search bar, Power BI Q&A automatically picks up the columns and calculated fields in the Excel data model and suggests how Jim can complete his question.

*Figure 6.55: Q&A makes suggestions about how to complete a question.*

Jim selects Sum of Revenue from the list of suggestions, and the answer shows up in the results.

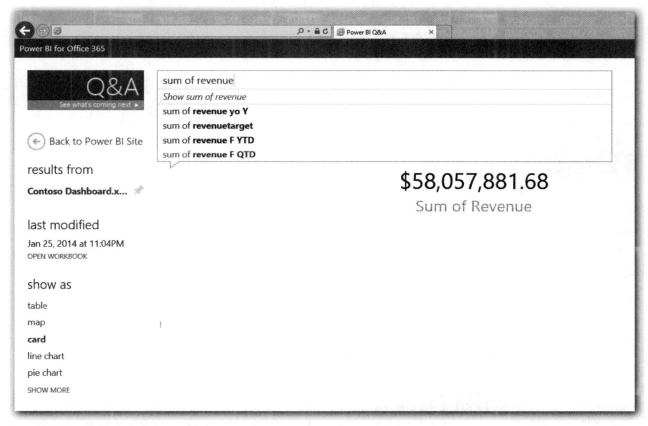

*Figure 6.56: Q&A results.*

Next, Jim refines the results by querying Sum of Revenue and RevenueTarget by State Name. Q&A automatically displays the right data visualization, based on the information the question returns.

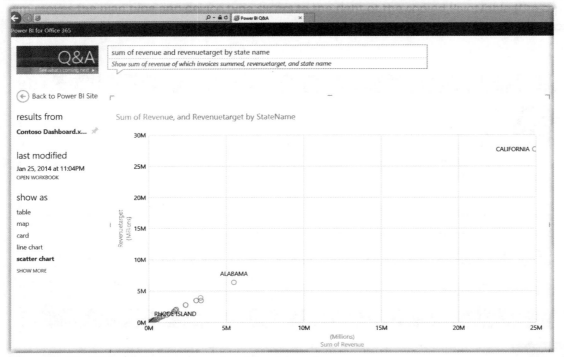

*Figure 6.57: Q&A results based on the data showed.*

Jim wants to change the way the data is displayed, so he selects Clustered Column Chart on the left side of the page.

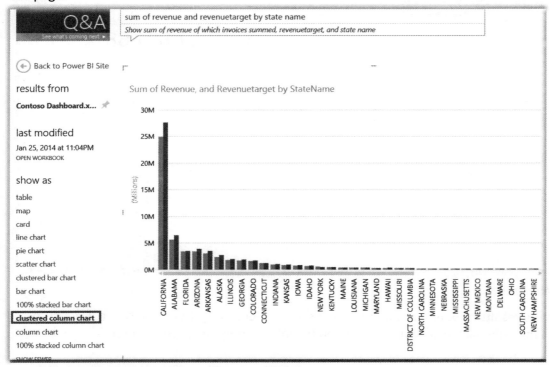

*Figure 6.58 Changing the Q&A data visualization.*

### Power BI Tip: Optimizing Q&A

You can optimize Q&A to allow much better search results by adding more semantic information. For more information, see this great help topic: http://ppivot.us/QyUOu.

Jim is now satisfied that he can start a proof of concept with his company, so he starts inviting his coworkers to the Power BI site to have them try it out.

# Bibliography and Suggested Readings

The following books provide more information on many of the topics discussed in this book.

On Power Pivot and DAX:

- Rob Collie, *DAX Formulas for PowerPivot: A Simple Guide to the Excel Revolution*, Holy Macro! Books (2012)

- Alberto Ferrari and Marco Russo, *Microsoft Excel 2013: Building Data Models with PowerPivot*, Microsoft Press (2013)

- Bill Jelen, *PowerPivot for the Data Analyst: Microsoft Excel 2010*, Que Publishing (2010)

Dashboarding and Data visualization:

- Stephen Few, *Information Dashboard Design: Displaying Data for At-a-Glance Monitoring*, 2nd ed., Analytics Press (2013)

- Edward R. Tufte, *The Visual Display of Quantitative Information*, 2nd ed., Graphics Pr (2001)

- Edward R. Tufte, *Beautiful Evidence*, Graphics Pr (2006)

Power View:

- Brian Larson, Mark Davis, Dan English, and Paul Purington, *Visualizing Data with Microsoft Power View*, McGraw-Hill Osborne Media (2012)

Power Pivot for SharePoint:

- Harinath, Pihlgren and Lee, *Professional Microsoft PowerPivot for Excel and SharePoint,* Wrox (2010)

- Warren, Teixeira Neto, Misner, Sanders, Helmers ,*Business Intelligence in Microsoft SharePoint 2013* Microsoft Press (2013)

The following are some Power Pivot blogs that are worth checking out:

- Rob Collie: http://www.powerpivotpro.com

- Bill Jelen (MrExcel): http://www.mrexcel.com

- Marco Russo and Alberto Ferrari: http://www.sqlbi.com

- Chandoo: http://chandoo.org

# Index of Tips

# Index

# POWERPIVOT
## Alchemy
### Patterns and Techniques for Excel

## Bill Jelen and Rob Collie

# DAX FORMULAS FOR PowerPivot

## The Excel Pro's Guide to Mastering DAX

**If you love Array Formulas, imagine combining the POWER of Array Formulas with MILLIONS of Rows of Data in Excel!**

**DAX is a NEW Function Language used to create calculated fields in Pivot Tables in Excel 2010 or Excel 2013 Pro Plus.**

**Learn how to leverage Powerful NEW Functions such as CALCULATE, RELATED, SUMX, DATESYTD, and many more with Rob Collie's book.**